MW00583035

Berlin Interiors
Intérieurs de Berlin

Photos
Eric Laignel
Production
Patricia Parinejad
Text
Ingeborg Wiensowski

Berlin Interiors
Intérieurs de Berlin

Edited by
Angelika Taschen

TASCHEN
KÖLN LONDON MADRID NEW YORK PARIS TOKYO

Vorsatz | Endpapers | Pages de garde:
Blick auf den Alexanderplatz, Berlin 1991
View of Alexanderplatz, Berlin 1991
Vue sur la Alexanderplatz, Berlin 1991
Photo: © Maik Jespersen/octopus/Bilderdienst Süddeutscher
Verlag, München
Seite 2 | Page 2:
Blick ins Schlafzimmer von Michel Würthle
View into the bedroom of Michel Würthle
La chambre à coucher de Michel Würthle
Seite 7 | Page 7:
Filmszene aus »Der blaue Engel« mit Marlene Dietrich, 1930
Film still from The Blue Angel with Marlene Dietrich, 1930
Une scène du film «L'Ange bleu», avec Marlene Dietrich, 1930
Photo: © Stiftung Deutsche Kinemathek – Marlene Dietrich
Collection Berlin
Seite 20/21 | Pages 20/21:
John F. Kennedy, Willy Brandt und Konrad Adenauer im Wagen
vor dem Brandenburger Tor, Berlin 26. Juni 1963
John F. Kennedy, Willy Brandt and Konrad Adenauer in the car at
the Brandenburg Gate, Berlin 26 June 1963
John F. Kennedy, Willy Brandt et Konrad Adenauer en voiture
devant la porte de Brandebourg, Berlin le 26 juin 1963
Photo: © Bildarchiv Preußischer Kulturbesitz, Berlin/Will
McBride
Seite 80/81 | Pages 80/81:
Sommertag auf einer Berliner Dachwiese, 1926
Summer's day on a grassy Berlin rooftop, 1926
Journée d'été sur un toit vert à Berlin, 1926
Photo: © Bildarchiv Preußischer Kulturbesitz, Berlin
Seite 110/111 | Pages 110/111:
»Meyers Hof« in der Ackerstraße, Berlin um 1935
Meyers Hof in Ackerstrasse, Berlin, around 1935
«Meyers Hof» dans la Ackerstrasse, Berlin vers 1935
Photo: © Berlinische Galerie, Berlin/Hennig Nolte
Seite 120/121 | Pages 120/121:
Berliner Hofmusikanten, um 1930
Berlin courtyard musicians, around 1930
Musiciens de cour, Berlin vers 1930
Photo:© Agentur für Bilder zur Zeitgeschichte, Berlin
Seite 160/161 | Pages 160/161:
Die Berliner Mauer, West-Berlin 1962
The Berlin Wall, West-Berlin 1962
Le Mur de Berlin, Berlin-Ouest 1962
Photo: © Henri Cartier-Bresson/Magnum Photos/Agentur Focus,
Hamburg
Seite 166/167 | Pages 166/167:
Ringelreihen auf dem Jüdenhof, Berlin um 1930
Ring-o-roses in the Jüdenhof, Berlin around 1930
Ronde sur le Jüdenhof, Berlin vers 1930
Photo: © Bildarchiv Preußischer Kulturbesitz, Berlin
Seite 182/183 | Pages 182/183:
Zugang zum U-Bahnhof Zoologischer Garten, Berlin-Charlotten-
burg 1912/1913
Entrance to the underground station Zoologischer Garten, Berlin-
Charlottenburg 1912/1913
Bouche de métro, station Zoologischer Garten, Berlin-Charlotten-
burg 1912/1913
Photo: © Archiv für Kunst und Geschichte, Berlin/P. A. Lebrun
Seite 198/199 | Pages 198/199:
Künstlerfest in Herwarth Waldens Galerie »Der Sturm«,
Berlin 1923

An artists' gathering at Herwarth Walden's gallery Der Sturm,
Berlin 1923
Fête des artistes à la galerie de Herwarth Walden «Der Sturm»,
Berlin 1923
Photo: © Bildarchiv Preußischer Kulturbesitz, Berlin
Seite 240/241 | Pages 240/241:
Auf einer Modenschau, Berlin um 1928
A fashion show in Berlin, around 1928
Défilé de mode à Berlin, vers 1928
Photo: © Hulton Archive/Getty Images, London
Seite 266/267 | Pages 266/267:
Trümmerfrauen tanzen zu Leierkastenmusik, Berlin 1945
Rubble clearance women dancing to the music of the hurdy-
gurdy, Berlin 1945
Les femmes qui déblaient le terrain dansent au son de l'orgue de
Barbarie, Berlin 1945
Photo: © Bildarchiv Preußischer Kulturbesitz, Berlin
Seite 288/289 | Pages 288/289:
Sonntagsausflug nach Werder, Berlin um 1900
A Sunday outing to Werder, Berlin around 1900
Excursion dominicale à Werder, Berlin vers 1900
Photo: © Bildarchiv Preußischer Kulturbesitz, Berlin/Otto
Haeckel
Seite 310/311 | Pages 310/311:
Zwei Badeschönheiten, Berlin 1920
Two bathing beauties, Berlin 1920
Deux sirènes, Berlin 1920
Photo: © Bildarchiv Preußischer Kulturbesitz, Berlin

© 2002 TASCHEN GmbH
Hohenzollernring 53, D–50672 Köln
www.taschen.com

© 2002 for the works by Ina Barfuss, Maria Eichhorn,
Mathis Esterhazy, Gretchen Faust, Robert Mangold,
Ludwig Mies van der Rohe, Hennig Nolte, Jean Prouvé,
Gerrit Rietveld, Thomas Ruff: VG Bild-Kunst, Bonn
© 2002 for the works by Le Corbusier: FLC/VG Bild-Kunst, Bonn
© 2002 for the works by Karl Blossfeldt: Karl Blossfeldt-Archiv/
Ann and Jürgen Wilde/VG Bild-Kunst, Bonn
© 2002 for the works by Charles and Ray Eames: Eames Office,
PO Box 268, Venice, CA 90294; www.eamesoffice.com

Edited and designed by Angelika Taschen, Cologne
Text edited by Susanne Klinkhamels, Cologne
Production by Horst Neuzner, Cologne
English translation by Michael Hulse, Golbach
French translation by Michèle Schreyer, Cologne

Printed in Spain
ISBN 3-8228-5885-4

Inhalt
Contents
Sommaire

construites, les barrières douanières disparaissent. Berlin est devenue une des premières villes industrielles du monde. La guerre suivante, qui voit la défaite de la France, l'ennemi héréditaire, conduit en 1871 à la fondation du Reich, avec Guillaume Ier comme premier empereur allemand. Il reste au pouvoir jusqu'en 1888, déclarée «l'année des trois empereurs»: en effet, Guillaume Ier meurt cette année-là, son successeur décède lui aussi 99 jours plus tard et Guillaume II prend sa suite – il sera le dernier Hohenzollern à monter sur le trône.

Lors de son couronnement, les Berlinois exultent, grisés par le patriotisme et la conscience d'habiter dans une ville d'importance mondiale. La capitale croît de jour en jour parce que des milliers de personnes vont y tenter leur chance malgré les crises économiques répétées. Les ouvriers arrivent à Berlin et s'installent dans les nouvelles «casernes locatives» (R.M. Rilke) de Wedding, Neukölln et Friedrichshain: des petits appartements aux loyers élevés, mal équipés sur le plan sanitaire et pourvus de jusqu'à six arrière-cours étroites en enfilade, dans lesquelles la voiture des pompiers peut à peu faire demi-tour. Des architectes progressistes comme Hermann Muthesius et Bruno Taut créent des lotissements de maisons mitoyennes et des cités-jardins pour les ouvriers, et ils construisent aussi quelques centaines de logements – une goutte d'eau dans la mer de la spéculation. La classe moyenne fortunée loue des maisons confortables à Charlottenburg où se trouve la nouvelle gare de la Savignyplatz. Ici, les occupants disposent d'au moins six pièces, chauffage central, salles de bains et une chambre de domestique. Les plus riches habitent dans des villas des faubourgs de Wannsee et Dahlem, par exemple. Des quartiers entiers sont consacrés à la banque, à la presse ou aux plaisirs. Les Berlinois appellent «Kaufstraße» (rue des acheteurs) la Leipziger Strasse avec ses grands magasins, le boulevard Unter den Linden est la «Laufstraße» (rue des piétons) et la Friedrichstraße est la «Saufstrasse» (rue des poivrots).

C'est l'époque des grands bals, à la cour aussi, et les gens vont aux concerts de Hans von Bülow, voient diriger les chefs d'orchestre Johannes Brahms, Richard Strauss et Gustav Mahler et écoutent chanter Enrico Caruso et Pablo Casals. Les premières théâtrales de Max Reinhardt au Deutsches Theater sont un événement mondain, au même titre que les représentations soporifiques à l'Opéra. Il y a aussi un orchestre qui joue du jazz et d'innombrables cabarets avec des chouchous du public tels Claire Waldoff dont le refrain «Hermann heeßt er» est repris par tout Berlin. Et puis on dîne en ville, élégamment chez Horcher ou au restaurant Rheingold qui peut accueillir 4000 personnes dans ses onze salles. Les deux buveurs notoires Edvard Munch et Knut Hansum vont rejoindre leur ami August Strindberg au Schwarzes Ferkel. Des artistes célèbres et des créateurs jeunes et inconnus, des marchands d'art, des galeristes comme Paul Cassirer et des gens importants des musées s'installent à Berlin.

Wohnung einer kinderreichen Familie, Berlin-Weißensee um 1907
Apartment of a large family, Berlin-Weißensee around 1907
L'appartement d'une famille nombreuse, Berlin-Weißensee vers 1907
Photo: © Archiv für Kunst und Geschichte, Berlin

Arbeitszimmer in der Villa von Carl Harteneck in Grunewald, Berlin 1913
The workroom in Carl Harteneck's villa in Grunewald, Berlin 1913
Bureau dans la villa de Carl Harteneck à Grunewald, Berlin 1913
Photo: © Ullstein Bild, Berlin/Waldemar Titzenthaler

Die berühmten »Sisters G«,
Berlin um 1925
The famous "Sisters G", Berlin
around 1925
Les célèbres «Sisters G», Berlin
vers 1925
Photo: © Getty Images,
London

Marlene Dietrich posiert für ein
Foto, Berlin 1935
Marlene Dietrich poses for a
photo, Berlin 1935
Marlene Dietrich prend la pose,
Berlin 1935
Photo: © Bildarchiv Preußi-
scher Kulturbesitz, Berlin

tropole, Industriestadt und Handelszentrum, denn für die
Großbetriebe war der Krieg ein gutes Geschäft gewesen.
Damals, zwischen 1919 und 1932, hatte die Stadt mehr als
vier Millionen Einwohner. Es waren die berühmten Zwan-
ziger Jahre, weltoffen, lebensfroh und liberal. Hier war der
Ort für Karrieren, denn eine feste, alteingesessene Gesellschaft gab es nicht mehr. Aber es gab noch die lebendige
Kulturszene, zu der auch der junge Carl Zuckmayer gehörte. Ihm »schmeckte Berlin nach Zukunft und dafür
nahm man den Dreck und die Kälte gern in Kauf«. Die
meisten der jungen Genies und Talente dachten ähnlich
und sie produzierten. Joseph Roth arbeitete als Journalist,
trank viel und schrieb nebenbei »Radetzkymarsch«. Am
Kudamm Ecke Fasanenstraße arbeitete Robert Musil an
seinem Roman »Der Mann ohne Eigenschaften«, Kurt
Tucholsky schrieb für die »Weltbühne« und veröffentlichte
zusammen mit John Heartfield 1929 »Deutschland,
Deutschland über alles«, Erich Kästner verdiente Geld
als Theaterkritiker und schrieb »Emil und die Detektive«,
Gottfried Benn praktizierte als Arzt und schrieb Gedichte
und Essays, Alfred Döblins »Berlin Alexanderplatz« er-
schien 1929, wurde zum Bestseller und schon 1931 ver-
filmt. Das war längst nicht alles. Die Umschlagplätze für
Wissen und Kommunikation waren nicht nur die 200 Ver-
lage, die 61 Morgen-, Mittags- und Abendzeitungen oder
die Galerien, es waren neuerdings die Künstlerlokale. An-
fangs traf man sich in dem legendären Café Größenwahn,
in dem Else Lasker-Schüler und ihr Mann Herwarth Walden
Stammgäste waren wie auch ihre Freunde Gottfried Benn,
Karl Kraus, Carl Einstein, Erich Mühsam oder Tilla Durieux.
Sie diskutierten nächtelang und entwarfen eine neue Welt.
Das konnte im Größenwahn ruhig etwas länger dauern,
»weil man bei einem Bier für 25 Pfennig die ganze Nacht
dort sitzen konnte, ohne vom Kellner ermahnt zu werden«.
Denn reich war fast keiner der Künstler und keiner wohnte
luxuriös. Machte nichts, denn »das Kaffeehaus ersparte
uns sozusagen eine Wohnung«, fand Egon Erwin Kisch.
Er saß oft im Café des Westens, umgeben von hübschen
jungen Mädchen. Später war das Romanische Café en
vogue. Die Atmosphäre war anders, denn auch die Boheme
war anders geworden. Es ging nicht mehr um Ideale, schrieb
Paul Marcus 1929, sondern es ging ums »Business«, weil
die Künstler ihr Geld als Fotografen, Kritiker und Film-
schauspieler verdienten. Und als Drehbuchautoren, denn
mit den expressionistischen Wunderwerken der Regie-
stars Ernst Lubitsch, Friedrich Wilhelm Murnau, Josef von
Sternberg und Fritz Lang und dem kommerziellen Erfolg
der Ufa waren die Filmstudios Babelsberg zu den größten
Studios Europas geworden. Stars wie Pola Negri, Marlene
Dietrich, Lilian Harvey oder Heinz Rühmann wurden hier
gemacht und Fritz Lang drehte 1925 seine Meisterwerke
»Metropolis«, »M« und »Das Testament des Dr. Mabuse«.
Im Ufa-Palast am Zoo wurden sie uraufgeführt vor über
2000 Zuschauern, und wenn nötig, begleitet vom hausei-
genen 75-Mann-Orchester. In Berlin gab es einfach alles:

cated, and the 14 years of the Weimar Republic that followed saw 20 governments and 13 chancellors. Berlin re-
mained the capital and a metropolitan centre of the arts,
trade and industry, since the war, after all, had been good
for big businesses. In the period from 1919 to 1932, the
city passed the four million population mark. The Roaring
Twenties were a time of easy-going, liberal-minded, open-
spirited *joie de vivre*. Berlin was a place where careers were
made, now that the old hide-bound fixed social structure
was vanishing. The arts scene was lively: to the young
writer Carl Zuckmayer, part of that scene, Berlin "tasted
of the future, and for that you gladly accepted the dirt and
cold". Most of the gifted young talents thought likewise –
and they were productive. Joseph Roth was a jobbing journalist and a heavy drinker but also wrote novels such as
Radetzky March. At the corner of Kurfürstendamm and
Fasanenstrasse, Robert Musil wrote his novel *The Man
Without Qualities*. Kurt Tucholsky wrote for the *Weltbühne*
an in 1929, with John Heartfield, published *Deutschland,
Deutschland über alles*. Erich Kästner earned a living as a
theatre critic but also wrote the children's classic *Emil and
the Detectives*. Gottfried Benn was in medical practice but
wrote his poems and essays on the side. Alfred Döblin's
Berlin Alexanderplatz was published in 1929, became a
best-seller, and was promptly filmed in 1931. And that was
not all. The arts were communicated not only through the
200 publishing houses, 61 morning, midday and evening
newspapers and the galleries, but also nowadays through
bars that attracted artistic clientele. There was the legendary Café Grössenwahn, for instance, where poet Else
Lasker-Schüler and her husband Herwarth Walden were
among the regulars along with their friends Gottfried
Benn, Karl Kraus, Carl Einstein, Erich Mühsam or Tilla
Durieux. Their discussions went on all night as they talked
a new world into being. Café Grössenwahn was a good
place for long sessions, too, "since you could nurse a 25
pfennig beer all night long without being pestered by the
waiter". Wealth was almost unknown among the artists,
and none led a life of luxury. Not that it mattered: "the
coffee-house spared us the need for a flat, as it were," to
quote writer Egon Erwin Kisch. He frequented the Café des
Westens, surrounded by pretty girls. Later the Romanisches Café was in vogue. The atmosphere was a different
one, for the bohemian scene had changed as well. Now,
wrote Paul Marcus in 1929, their concern was no longer
with ideals, it was with business. Artists earned a living as
photographers, critics and movie actors. They also wrote
screenplays: the outstanding achievements of Expression-
ist cinema, created by star directors such as Ernst Lubitsch,
Friedrich Wilhelm Murnau, Josef von Sternberg and Fritz
Lang, together with the commercial success of the Ufa,
had made the Babelsberg studios the biggest in Europe.
Stars such as Pola Negri, Marlene Dietrich, Lilian Harvey
or Heinz Rühmann were made there, and in 1925 Fritz
Lang made his masterpieces *Metropolis*, *M* and the *Dr.*

Après la Première Guerre mondiale, un nouvel Etat voit le jour. Le Kaiser abdique et, les 14 années qui suivent seront celles de la République de Weimar avec 20 gouvernements et 13 chanceliers. Berlin reste la capitale et la métropole culturelle, la ville industrielle et le centre de commerce car la guerre a été profitable aux grandes entreprises. Entre 1919 et 1932, la ville compte plus de quatre millions d'habitants – ce sont les fameuses Années folles avec leur ouverture sur le monde, leur joie de vivre et leur libéralisme. C'est ici que l'on fait carrière car il n'existe plus à Berlin de société solide, ancrée depuis longtemps. Mais la scène culturelle, elle, est encore bien vivante, et le jeune Carl Zuckmayer en fait aussi partie. Pour lui «Berlin avait le goût d'avenir et on s'accommodait volontiers en retour de la saleté et du froid». Une opinion que partagent la plupart des jeunes génies ou des talents en éclosion et ils sont très productifs. Joseph Roth est journaliste, boit beaucoup et écrit dans son temps libre «La Marche de Radetzky». Sur le «Kudamm», au coin de la Fasanenstrasse, Robert Musil travaille à son roman «L'homme sans qualités»; Kurt Tucholsky est rédacteur à l'hebdomadaire «Weltbühne» et fait paraître avec John Heartfield en 1929 l'album «Deutschland, Deutschland über alles», Erich Kästner gagne de l'argent comme critique de théâtre et écrit «Emile et les détectives», Gottfried Benn est médecin et écrit des poèmes et des essais; le «Berlin Alexanderplatz» d'Alfred Döblin paraît en 1929, devient un best-seller et est porté à l'écran dès 1931. Mais l'énumération est loin d'être complète. Les plaques tournantes du savoir et de la communication ne sont pas seulement les 200 maisons d'édition, les 61 quotidiens paraissant le matin, le midi ou le soir ou les galeries – les cafés artistiques ont maintenant aussi un rôle à jouer. Au début, les artistes se réunissent dans des établissements comme le Café Größenwahn, où Else Lasker-Schüler et son mari Herwarth Walden sont des habitués et rencontrent leurs amis Gottfried Benn, Karl Kraus, Carl Einstein, Erich Mühsam ou Tilla Durieux. Ils discutent des nuits entières et refont le monde – il faut dire qu'on peut rester ici assis toute la nuit devant une bière à 25 pfennig sans que le serveur ne s'affole. Car les artistes qui roulent sur l'or sont rares et aucun n'habite un appartement luxueux. Aucune importance, vu que «le café nous économise un logement», trouve Egon Erwin Kisch qui séjourne souvent au Café des Westens, entouré de jolies filles. Plus tard, c'est le Romanisches Café qui sera à la mode; l'atmosphère y est différente car la bohème a changé. Il n'est alors plus question d'idéaux, ainsi que l'écrit Paul Marcus en 1929, mais de «business», car les artistes gagnent leur vie comme photographes, critiques et acteurs de cinéma. Et aussi comme scénaristes, car les merveilles expressionnistes des réalisateurs de génie que sont Ernst Lubitsch, Friedrich Wilhelm Murnau, Josef von Sternberg et Fritz Lang et le succès commercial de l'UFA, ont fait des studios cinématographiques de Babelsberg les plus grands d'Eu-

Kino am Vahamorf Platz, Berlin 1927
The cinema at Vahamorf Platz, Berlin 1927
Le cinéma de la Vahamorf Platz, Berlin 1927
Photo: © Getty Images, London

Nachtclub mit Tanzfläche und Schwimmbad, Berlin um 1935
A nightclub with dance floor and swimming pool, Berlin around 1935
Boîte de nuit avec piste de danse et piscine, Berlin vers 1935
Photo: © Getty Images, London

Boykottaufruf auf dem Schaufenster einer Drogerie, Berlin 1933
A call to boycott, on a drugstore window, Berlin 1933
Appel au boycottage sur la vitrine d'une droguerie, Berlin 1933
Photo: © Bildarchiv Preußischer Kulturbesitz, Berlin

Zum Auftakt der Olympiade fährt Hitler ins Olympiastadion ein, Berlin 1936
Hitler driving into the Olympic Stadium for the opening of the Olympic Games, Berlin 1936
L'ouverture des Jeux Olympiques: Hitler arrive dans le stade, Berlin 1936
Photo: © Coll. H. Chr. Adam, Göttingen/Max Ehlert

Piscator machte Revolutionstheater, ein paar junge Talente inszenierten »Die Dreigroschenoper«, dass die Wände wackelten, und im Domgottesdienst rief ein Dadaist schon mal laut »Jesus Christus ist uns wurscht«. Ab und zu wurde ein Prominenter mit Kokain erwischt oder einer der vielen gleichgeschlechtlichen Clubs geschlossen. Architekten wie Ludwig Mies van der Rohe entwarfen gläserne Hochhäuser und bauten unter der Leitung von Bruno Taut und Hugo Häring 1926–1932 »Onkel Toms Hütte«, eine vorbildliche Siedlung mit 809 Einfamilienhäusern.

Erich Kästner gehörte zu den Künstlern mit unheilvollen Ahnungen. 1930 hatte er einen Wunsch an den Weihnachtsmann in der »Weltbühne« veröffentlicht: »Und nach München lenk die Schritte, wo der Hitler wohnen soll. Hau dem Guten, bitte, bitte, den Germanenhintern voll.« Seine Ahnung bestätigte sich schnell: Im Januar 1933 marschierten die Nazis durchs Brandenburger Tor. Schon ein paar Monate später wurden jüdische Geschäfte boykottiert und Bücher öffentlich verbrannt. Trotzdem fanden drei Jahre später in Berlin die Olympischen Spiele statt. Die meisterhafte Inszenierung begeisterte drei Millionen Besucher aus aller Welt, die politische Situation kümmerte kaum einen der Sportfans. Für die Nationalsozialisten waren die Spiele nicht nur ein Image-Erfolg: Deutschland gewann die Nationenwertung. Nur im Fußball ging alles schief. Im einzigen Spiel, das Hitler jemals besuchte, verlor Deutschland gegen Norwegen 2:0. Eine kleine Schlappe, er träumte sowieso von anderen Aufgaben: Berlin sollte zu »Germania« als Hauptstadt eines großgermanischen Weltreiches umgebaut werden. »Wenn Völker große Zeiten innerlich erleben, so gestalten sie diese Zeiten auch äußerlich um.«

Das tat er dann auch. Deutschland und Berlin versanken in Schutt und Asche. Von den 160 000 Berliner Juden überlebten 5000. Alle hungerten und froren. Sie holzten den Tiergarten für Brennholz ab und bauten dort Kartoffeln an. Dann gab es »Trümmerfrauen«, zwei deutsche Staaten und einen Kalten Krieg. Der eskalierte, als im Westen die Währungsreform durchgeführt wurde. Die Sowjets blockierten alle Zufahrten nach Berlin, die Amerikaner versorgten die Stadt durch die Luft. »Rosinenbomber« nannten die Berliner die Flugzeuge. Fast ein ganzes Jahr dauerte das Drama. Danach ging es wieder aufwärts.

Der Westen baute 1955–1957 das Hansaviertel mit internationalen Architektenstars wie Oscar Niemeyer, Alvar Aalto, Walter Gropius, Max Taut, Egon Eiermann und Le Corbusier, der Osten die Stalinallee mit 2000 Wohnungen im sozialistischen Zuckerbäcker-Stil. Aber die DDR blutete aus – Millionen verließen das Land, auch die geistige Elite. Deshalb ließ der Ministerrat 1961 die Mauer bauen. 155 Kilometer lang, mit beleuchtetem Todesstreifen und Wachtürmen. Die Stadt stand unter Schock. Da half es auch nicht, dass John F. Kennedy 1963 öffentlich erklärte: »Ich bin ein Berliner«. Berlin versank langsam in Bedeutungslosigkeit. Viele Berliner zogen nach West-

Mabuse films. The fact was that Berlin simply had everything: Piscator was doing revolutionary theatre, a couple of gifted youngsters named Brecht and Weill mounted a show called *The Threepenny Opera* that shook the very rafters, and during one service in the cathedral a Dadaist shouted out "We don't care about Jesus Christ." From time to time some prominent personality would be caught in possession of cocaine, or one of the numerous gay clubs would be closed down. Architects such as Mies van der Rohe were designing high-rises made of glass and from 1926 to 1932 Uncle Tom's Cabin, a model development of 809 family homes, was built under the direction of Bruno Taut and Hugo Häring.

Erich Kästner was one of the artists, writers and intellectuals who suspected what was coming. In 1930 in the *Weltbühne* he published his request to Father Christmas: "Santa, go to Munich, please: / Hitler, I'm told, doth there abide. / Get him down upon his knees / And leather his Germanic hide." His suspicions soon proved justified: in January 1933 the Nazis marched through the Brandenburg Gate. Within months, Jewish shops were being boycotted and books burnt in public. Nevertheless, three years later, the Olympics were held in Berlin. A dazzling show for over three million sports fans from around the world; precious few took interest in the political situation at hand. For the Nazis, the games were of course not merely good for their image, they were good in sporting terms: Germany ranked first among the competing nations, and only in soccer did German aims fall short. In the only match Hitler ever attended, Germany was beaten by Norway 2:0. But this minor mishap was of little consequence, since Hitler had quite other dreams: Berlin was to be transformed into "Germania", the capital of a global Greater German Reich. "When a people has a real inner experience of great times, it will re-shape those times in outer form as well."

Hitler certainly did that. Along with much of Europe, Germany and Berlin were left in rubble. When the Second World War ended, just 5,000 of Berlin's 160,000 Jews had survived. The entire population was cold and starving. The trees in the zoo were felled for firewood and potatoes planted instead. This was the time of the "Trümmerfrauen", the women of the rubble; and of two German states, and the Cold War, which escalated when the currency was reformed in the Western-occupied sectors. The Soviets blockaded all access to Berlin, and the Americans and British supplied the city from the air, in the celebrated "air bridge", a dramatic operation that was kept up for almost a year. Subsequently Berlin began to recover.

From 1955 to 1957 West Berlin rebuilt the Hansaviertel, employing international star architects such as Oscar Niemeyer, Alvar Aalto, Walter Gropius, Max Taut, Egon Eiermann and Le Corbusier, while East Berlin built Stalinallee, lined with 2,000 homes in the confectionery style favoured by the Communists. In fact, the GDR was bleeding to death; millions were voting with their feet,

rope. C'est ici qu'ont été créées des stars comme Pola Negri, Marlene Dietrich ou Heinz Rühmann et c'est ici que Fritz Lang tourne en 1925 ses chefs-d'œuvre «Metropolis», «M le Maudit» et «Le Testament du Dr Mabuse». A Berlin, on trouve de tout: Piscator fait du théâtre révolutionnaire, quelques jeunes talents mettent en scène «l'Opéra de quat'sous» que les murs en tremblent, et dans la cathédrale pendant la messe, un dadaïste s'écrie une fois «Jésus-Christ on s'en tape». De temps en temps, une personnalité se fait pincer avec une ligne de coco ou on ferme un des nombreux clubs homosexuels. Les architectes comme Ludwig Mies van der Rohe créent des immeubles de verre et construisent sous la direction de Bruno Taut et Hugo Häring «La case de l'oncle Tom» (1926–1932), un lotissement comprenant 809 maisons.

Erich Kästner fait partie de ces artistes qui ont des pressentiments funestes. Dès 1930, il publie dans la «Weltbühne» un vœu au père Noël: «Et guide les pas de Hitler vers Munich, c'est là qu'il doit habiter. Et s'il te plaît, s'il te plaît botte à ce bonhomme son derrière germanique.» Il ne sera pas exaucé: en janvier 1933, les nazis défilent sous la Porte de Brandebourg. Quelques mois plus tard des magasins juifs sont boycottés et les livres brûlés en public. Ce qui n'empêchera pas les Jeux Olympiques de se dérouler à Berlin trois ans plus tard et d'enthousiasmer trois millions de visiteurs du monde entier par leur mise en scène magistrale. La situation politique ne préoccupe guère les accros du sport. Pour les nationaux-socialistes, les Jeux renforcent l'image de l'Allemagne puisque celle-ci est en tête du classement des nations. Seul le football est navrant. Dans le seul match auquel Hitler assistera jamais, l'Allemagne perd contre la Norvège – 2 à 0. Il se remet facilement de ce camouflet car il a des projets plus ambitieux: Berlin doit devenir «Germania», la capitale d'un empire pangermanique. «Quand des peuples vivent intérieurement de grandes époques, ils transforment aussi ces époques extérieurement».

Il tiendra parole. Après la guerre, l'Allemagne et Berlin ne sont plus que l'ombre d'elles-mêmes. Des 160 000 juifs berlinois, 5000 ont survécu. Tout le monde a faim et froid. Les gens abattent les arbres du Tiergarten pour faire du feu et y cultivent des pommes de terre. Des femmes courageuses s'attaquent aux décombres. Puis vient le temps des deux Etats allemands et de la guerre froide qui s'intensifie quand les secteurs occidentaux adoptent la réforme monétaire. Les Soviets bloquent tous les accès à Berlin – les Américains ravitaillent la ville à l'aide d'avions cargos que les Berlinois appellent les «bombardiers de raisins secs». La tragédie durera près d'un an, ensuite la ville reprend le dessus.

De 1955 à 1957, le Hansaviertel est construit à l'Ouest par des architectes stars comme Oscar Niemeyer, Alvar Aalto, Walter Gropius, Max Taut, Egon Eiermann et Le Corbusier, à l'Est on aménage la Stalinallee avec 2000 appartements, style «gâteau de mariée» socialiste. Mais

Jubelnde BDM-Mädchen erwarten Adolf Hitler, Berlin 16. März 1938
Cheering BDM-girls awaiting Adolf Hitler, Berlin March 16, 1938
Les jeunes filles du BDM attendent Adolf Hitler dans l'allégresse, Berlin le 16 mars 1938
Photo: © Bildarchiv Preußischer Kulturbesitz, Berlin/Arthur Grimm

Die zerstörte Kaiser-Wilhelm-Gedächtniskirche, Berlin 1945
Ruin of the Kaiser-Wilhelm-Gedächtniskirche, Berlin 1945
L'église commémorative Kaiser-Wilhelm détruite, Berlin 1945
Photo: © Robert Capa/Magnum Photos/Agentur Focus, Hamburg

*Siegessäule aus der Vogel-
perspektive, West-Berlin 1961
Bird's-eye view of the Victory
Column, West-Berlin 1961
La colonne de la Victoire vue
à vol d'oiseau, Berlin-Ouest 1961
Photo: © Rene Burri/Magnum
Photos/Agentur Focus,
Hamburg*

deutschland, die Neuberliner kamen aus der Provinz, es entstand eine Kleinbürgerschicht. Kein Wunder, Karrieren waren hier nicht zu machen. Das produktive Kapital war aus Berlin abgewandert, keine Banken, keine Industrie, keine gute Gesellschaft. Aber jede Menge Bauskandale, drittklassige Politiker mit Schrebergärten und staatlich geförderte Künstler. Und Buletten mit Mostrich und Soleier auf Empfängen.

Bunt und laut war es trotzdem in Berlin, die Stadt war immer noch groß und hatte Platz für demonstrierende Studenten, Hausbesetzer, Punks und die neuen türkischen Berliner. Am Kudamm war es nach wie vor großstädtisch. Hier wurde eingekauft, gewohnt, ausgegangen, gearbeitet. Gebaut wurde auch wieder, aber nicht mehr mit Architektenstars. Berliner Lokalmatadore entwarfen spießige Siedlungen oder gigantische Satellitenstädte wie das Märkische Viertel und die Gropius-Stadt.

In den 1980er Jahren gab sich West-Berlin wieder hauptstädtischer: Neue Deutsche Welle, Wilde Malerei, wilde Clubs und Großausstellungen. Und jedes Jahr am 1. Mai rüstete sich die alternative Szene zur Schlacht in Kreuzberg unter dem originellen Motto »haut die Bullen platt wie Stullen«. Das Westfernsehen war immer dabei. Im Osten waren die 1. Mai-Demonstrationen ordentlich. In Reih und Glied wurde am Staatsratsvorsitzenden vorbeimarschiert, dort, wo mal das Schloss gestanden hatte. Und die Nationalhymne wurde gesungen »Auferstanden aus Ruinen ...«. Der Ost-Berliner wusste, was er nicht hatte, weil er Westfernsehen empfangen konnte. Das trug zur Unzufriedenheit und zum Rückzug ins Private bei. Man pflegte seinen Schrebergarten und die jungen Intellektuellen trafen sich in ihren Wohnungen im Prenzlauer Berg. Dann ging man zu Kundgebungen, ohne zu ahnen, dass man an der ersten friedlichen Revolution in Deutschland teilnahm.

Als die Mauer dann fiel, kam alles raus: Honecker hatte Westarmaturen in seinen Bädern, RAF-Mitglieder hatten in der DDR gelebt, die Stasi hatte fast jeden bespitzelt, Olympiasieger waren gedopt. Und im Westen kriegte man nach dem Begrüßungsgeld nie wieder was geschenkt. Aber wie sagt der Berliner? »Uns kann keener.«

leaving the country, among them the intellectual elite. In response, the council of ministers had the Wall built, in 1961. It was 155 kilometres long, with a brightly-lit death-strip and watch-towers. The city was in a state of shock. It was of no avail if President John F. Kennedy proclaimed publicly in 1963 that he was "ein Berliner". Many Berliners moved to West Germany, while those newly moving to the city were provincials; the result was a *petit bourgeois city*, and small wonder, since there was no making a career there. Productive capital had quit Berlin, there were neither banks nor industry nor society. Instead there were any number of building scandals, there were third-rate politicians who tended their allotment gardens, and there were state-subsidized artists. And at buffet receptions there were meat balls with mustard and pickled eggs.

Life in Berlin was a bright and bustling affair nevertheless. It was still a big city, and there was room enough for student demonstrators, squatters, punks and the new Turkish citizens of the city. Kurfürstendamm was a metropolitan boulevard as it always had been. Construction work continued, though no longer with star architects. Berlin's locally prominent names designed dreary estates or gigantic satellite towns such as the Märkisches Viertel or Gropius-Stadt.

In the 1980s, West Berlin began to feel more like a capital again, with the Neue Deutsche Welle (German New Wave) in rock music, the art of the Neue Wilden (New Fauves), wild clubs, and major exhibitions. And on May 1st of every year, the "alternative scene" girded its loins for battle in Kreuzberg, chanting war-cries against the police. West German television invariably covered the street-fighting. In East Berlin, the First of May demonstrations proceeded in an orderly manner, parading in ranks past the city councillors on the very spot where once the palace had stood and singing the national anthem, the East German version of which began with the words "Auferstanden aus Ruinen ..." (Arisen from the ruins). The people of East Berlin well knew what they were missing, since they could watch West German television. This only augmented their dissatisfaction and encouraged a retreat into the private sphere. They tended their allotment gardens. The young intellectuals gathered in their apartments in Prenzlauer Berg. And presently they began going to public assemblies, without suspecting that they were participating in Germany's first peaceful revolution.

And then when the Wall fell, out came all the secrets: Erich Honecker had western fittings in his bathrooms, members of the Red Army Faction terrorist group had lived in the GDR, the Stasis had spied on practically everyone, Olympic winners were doped. As for those who went West from the East, once they'd received a "welcome payment" there were no more freebies. But then, the people of Berlin do say, "No one fools us".

la RDA est saignée à blanc – des millions de personnes quittent le pays et aussi l'élite intellectuelle. Le conseil ministériel veut stopper l'hémorragie et Ulbricht fait édifier en 1961 une construction de 155 km de long avec zones «danger de mort» éclairées et tours de surveillance: le mur de Berlin. La ville est sous le choc. John F. Kennedy a beau déclarer publiquement en 1963 «Ich bin ein Berliner», cela n'y change rien. De nombreux Berlinois quittent la ville et s'installent en Allemagne de l'Ouest. Quant aux nouveaux venus, ils viennent de province et on voit apparaître une classe de petits-bourgeois – ce qui n'a rien d'étonnant, le mot «carrière» étant inconnu ici. Le capital productif a quitté Berlin – plus de banques, plus d'industries, plus de bonne société, mais des scandales de construction en veux-tu en voilà, des politiciens médiocres avec jardin ouvrier et des artistes soutenus par l'Etat.

Néanmoins Berlin reste colorée et bruyante, la ville est toujours vaste, elle a de la place pour les étudiants contestataires, les squatters, les punks et les nouveaux Berlinois turcs. La grande ville, on la trouve encore sur le Kurfürstendamm. On recommence à construire. Des matadors de quartiers conçoivent des lotissements conformistes ou des villes-satellites gigantesques comme le Märkische Viertel ou la Gropius-Stadt.

Au cours des années 1980, Berlin-Ouest se souvient de son rôle de capitale: Neue Deutsche Welle (Nouvelle Vague allemande), Neue Wilde (peinture «sauvage»), clubs échevelés et grandes expositions. Et tous les 1er mai, les alternatifs sont au rendez-vous à Kreuzberg, prêts à en découdre avec les forces de l'ordre en suivant la consigne originale «Aplatissez les flics comme des galettes». La télévision ouest-allemande est toujours bien présente. A l'Est, les manifs du 1er mai sont vraiment très comme il faut: on défile en rangs serrés devant les présidents du conseil d'Etat. Et on entonne l'hymne national qui parle de ruines et de résurrection.

Le Berlinois de l'Est est bien conscient de tout ce qu'il rate. Cela génère bien des frustrations et un repli sur le privé. Les gens cultivent leur jardin ouvrier et les jeunes intellectuels se réunissent dans leurs appartements du Prenzlauer Berg. Et puis ils iront aux manifestations sans se rendre compte qu'ils participent à la première révolution pacifique en Allemagne.

Après la chute du Mur, on découvre que Honecker avait fait venir les robinets de sa salle de bains d'Allemagne de l'Ouest, que des membres de la RAF avaient vécu à l'Est, que la Stasi a pratiquement espionné tout le monde et que les athlètes vainqueurs aux J. O. étaient dopés. Quant à l'Ouest, une fois la prime d'accueil déboursée, il ne fait pas de cadeaux. Qu'importe, le Berlinois ne se démonte pas pour si peu – «Uns kann keener» dit-il, formule lapidaire qui signifie à peu près que rien ne saurait entamer sa confiance en lui-même et en l'avenir.

Der Lehrter Bahnhof im Bau, Berlin 2000
The Lehrter train station under construction, Berlin 2000
La gare de Lehrt en chantier, Berlin 2000
Photo: © Karl-Ludwig Lange, Berlin

Berlin bei Nacht: Philharmonie und Potsdamer Platz mit Sony Center, Berlin 2000
Berlin by night: The Berlin Philharmonic and Potsdamer Platz with Sony Center, Berlin 2000
Berlin la nuit: la Philharmonie et la Potsdamer Platz avec le Sony Center, Berlin 2000
Photo: © Ian Berry/Magnum Photos/Agentur Focus, Hamburg

Berlin-Mitte

There were estate agents who swore Paul Maenz wasn't quite right in the head when he told them which part of town he was looking for a flat in. And yet the solution was perfectly simple. Because what the former Cologne art dealer was looking for existed only in one area of Berlin: "I wanted to be in the historic centre, I wanted the whole Berlin thing," says Maenz. And that is precisely where he is now living. "This flat is an idea. Everything that has constituted our history is present here in symbolic form." 22 doors open onto the balcony, which runs all around the flat, with views of the Brandenburg Gate, the Victory Column, the zoo, Potsdamer Platz and the towers of the Gendarmenmarkt. Indeed, it is impossible to have more of Berlin anywhere else. When a million ravers get together for Berlin's Love Parade or New Year celebrations on his own front door, when some state visitor glides by, or Japanese take their positions for a photo, Maenz is enthusiastic and talks of a democratic forum, taking delight in it all: "This location really is unique in the whole world."

Paul Maenz

Einige Makler tippten sich an die Stirn, wenn Paul Maenz ihnen erklärte, in welcher Gegend er eine Wohnung suchte. Dabei wäre es ganz einfach gewesen, denn das, was der ehemalige Kölner Galerist suchte, gibt es nur einmal in Berlin: »Ich wollte in die historische Mitte, ich wollte Berlin total«, sagt Maenz. Und da genau lebt er jetzt. »Diese Wohnung ist eine Idee, alles, was unsere Geschichte ausmacht, ist als Symbol vorhanden.« 22 Türen führen auf den umlaufenden Balkon, der den Blick eröffnet auf das Brandenburger Tor, die Siegessäule, den Tiergarten, den Potsdamer Platz und die Türme des Gendarmenmarktes. Von einem demokratischen Forum schwärmt Maenz, wenn sich vor seiner Tür eine Million Raver zur Love-Parade treffen, wenn ein Staatsbesuch vorbeirauscht oder Japaner für ein Foto Aufstellung nehmen. Das freut Maenz. »Weil es diesen Platz wirklich nur einmal auf der Welt gibt.«

Quand Paul Maenz leur expliqua dans quel endroit il cherchait un logement, certains agents immobiliers le prirent pour un fou. Pourtant, ce n'était pas bien compliqué: «Je voulais le cœur historique, Berlin total», dit Maenz, ex-propriétaire de galerie à Cologne. Et c'est là qu'il vit aujourd'hui. «Tout ce qui fait notre histoire est présent dans cet appartement en tant que symbole». 22 portes mènent au balcon qui fait le tour de la maison et duquel on peut voir la Porte de Brandebourg, la colonne de la Victoire, le Tiergarten (le parc zoologique), la place de Potsdam et les tours du Gendarmenmarkt. Maenz est transporté, parle de forum démocratique quand se déroule la Love Parade et que plus d'un million de ravers se retrouvent devant sa porte, quand on fête la Saint-Sylvestre, quand passe le cortège d'un chef d'Etat en visite ou quand des Japonais prennent la pose pour la photo souvenir. Tout cela enchante Maenz. «Cet endroit-là est vraiment unique au monde.»

Vorhergehende Doppelseite: Beim Frühstück auf seinem Balkon sieht Paul Maenz das Brandenburger Tor, den Potsdamer Platz, den Tiergarten und die Siegessäule.
Rechts: Im Eingang steht Gerrit Rietvelds Stuhl »Zig-Zag« von 1910, der später in Serie hergestellt wurde.
Unten: Vor einer Spiegelmosaikwand des Schweizers John Armleder lehnt ein Fahrrad vom italienischen Künstler Mauricio Cattelan. An der Wand eine Fotoarbeit von Thomas Ruff.

Previous pages: When he has breakfast on his balcony, Paul Maenz has a view of the Brandenburg Gate, Potsdamer Platz, Tiergarten and the Victory Column.
Right: In the hall is Gerrit Rietveld's 1910 "Zig-Zag" chair, which later went into serial production.
Below: The mirror mosaic wall is by Switzerland's John Armleder, the bicycle leaning against it by Italian artist Mauricio Cattelan. The photograph on the wall is by Thomas Ruff.

Double page précédente: De son balcon, Paul Maenz voit la porte de Brandebourg, la Place de Potsdam, le Tiergarten et la colonne de la Victoire.
A droite: Dans l'entrée, la chaise «Zig-Zag» créée en 1910 par Gerrit Rietveld, et plus tard fabriquée en série.
Ci-dessous: devant un mur en mosaïque de miroir du Suisse John Armleder, une bicyclette de l'artiste italien Mauricio Cattelan. Au mur, une photographie de Thomas Ruff.

Oben: *Seine kleine Privatausstellung räumt der ehemalige Galerist oft um. Vor dem Gemälde »Jeune femme etonnée« von Julien Michel steht der Stuhl »Berlin« von Rietveld, davor liegen zwei Objekte von Elmgren und Dragset wie achtlos ausgezogene Jeans.*
Rechts: *Tisch und Sideboard sind eine Sonderanfertigung für Maenz.*

Above: *Maenz, formerly an art dealer, frequently re-hangs his private exhibition. The painting is Julien Michel's "Jeune femme etonnée" and the chair is Rietveld's "Berlin" chair, and on the floor, looking like discarded jeans, are two objects by Elmgren and Dragset.*
Right: *The table and sideboard were handmade by a carpenter.*

Ci-dessus: *L'ex-galeriste change souvent de place les objets de sa collection personnelle. Devant le tableau «Jeune femme étonnée» signé Julien Michel, la chaise «Berlin» de Rietveld. Sur le sol, tels deux jeans négligemment ôtés, deux objets d'Elmgren et Dragset.*
A droite: *Un menuisier a réalisé la table et le dressoir.*

Linke Seite: im Wohnzimmer ein Sofa von Antonio Citterio. Das Bild hat Gerwald Rockenschaub eigens für die Wand gemacht. Die afrikanischen Skulpturen hat Maenz schon zu Studienzeiten gesammelt.
Oben und rechts: Wohn-, Esszimmer und Ausstellungsraum gehen ineinander über. Ein Fernrohr für den klaren Weitblick.
Folgende Doppelseite: Details aus Flur, Wohnzimmer, Schrankzimmer, Bad und Küche.

Facing page: In the living room is a sofa by Antonio Citterio. The painting was created by Gerwald Rockenschaub especially for this wall. Maenz began collecting African sculptures back in his student days.
Above and right: The living and dining rooms and exhibition space are seamlessly connected. The telescope serves to enjoy the far views.
Following pages: details of the hall, living room, dressing room, bathroom and kitchen.

Page de gauche: dans le séjour, un sofa d'Antonio Citterio, un tableau signé Gerwald Rockenschaub, spécialement conçu pour le mur. Etudiant, Maenz collectionnait déjà les statues africaines.
Ci-dessus et à droite: Le séjour, la salle à manger et l'espace d'exposition sont en enfilade. Un télescope pour ne rien perdre du panorama.
Double page suivante: des détails du couloir, du séjour, du dressing, de la salle de bains et de la cuisine.

In 1837, when Czar Nicholas was planning to purchase the rococo number 7, Unter den Linden, in Berlin, he first had to be declared an honorary citizen, since foreigners were not permitted to own land. As soon as he was the owner, he had Russian soil moved to the site. And so the building stood on the soil of the motherland, until it was demolished in 1942 and rebuilt in 1953 as the Soviet Embassy, with a frontage away from the street side, a ceremonial courtyard, and a central tract resembling a tower. "Stalinist classicism" is the term critics use for this pomp-ridden architectural style, which makes any petitioner feel small the moment he enters the majestic stairwell. Today the building is the Russian Embassy, and much has changed. "Our diplomatic aim nowadays is to steer public opinion towards Russia in a positive direction," says ambassador Sergei Krylov. Hence the lectures, conferences, concerts and festivities on the premises. The ornate decor with its glass, gold and encrustations suits this new approach far better than political ends.

Russische Botschaft

Als Zar Nikolaus 1837 für seine Diplomatie das Rokoko-Haus Unter den Linden 7 kaufen wollte, musste er zuerst zum Ehrenbürger ernannt werden, denn Ausländer durften keinen Berliner Boden erwerben. Den wollte Nikolaus auch gar nicht. Kaum war er Eigentümer, ließ er russische Erde herbeikarren. Bis 1942 stand das Haus auf dem Mutterboden, dann fiel es in Schutt und Asche. 1953 wurde es wieder aufgebaut, als Botschaft der Sowjetunion in der DDR. Mit zurückliegender Front, Ehrenhof und turmähnlichem Mittelbau. »Stalinistischen Klassizismus« nennen Kritiker den pompösen Baustil, der einen Bittsteller schon im prunkvollen Treppenhaus klein macht. Jetzt ist die Botschaft russisch und vieles ist anders. »Heute will die Diplomatie die öffentliche Meinung zu Russland positiv beeinflussen«, sagt Botschafter Sergey Krylov. Deshalb gibt es Vorträge, Konferenzen, Konzerte und Feste im Haus. Dazu passen der Zuckerbäcker-Zierrat, Glas und Gold viel besser als zur Politik.

Quand le tsar Nicolas Ier voulut acheter la maison rococo du 7 Unter den Linden, il fallut le nommer citoyen d'honneur parce que les étrangers ne devaient pas prendre possession du sol berlinois. Ce n'était manifestement pas son intention: à peine propriétaire, il fit acheminer des tonnes de terre russe. La maison resta ainsi sur la terre mère jusqu'en 1942, après il n'en resta que des décombres. En 1953, elle fut reconstruite en tant qu'Ambassade de l'Union soviétique en RDA. «Néoclassique stalinien», c'est ainsi que les critiques ont baptisé ce style pompeux – les solliciteurs qui montent l'escalier prennent conscience de leur insignifiance. Maintenant l'ambassade est russe et bien des choses ont changé. «Aujourd'hui, la diplomatie veut influencer positivement le public», dit l'ambassadeur Sergeï Krylov, et c'est la raison pour laquelle on organise ici des conférences, des concerts et des fêtes. Les ornements style gâteau de mariage, le verre et l'or s'y prêtent mieux qu'à la politique.

Eingangsseite: Wappensaal mit blattvergoldeten Wandkapitellen und den Wappen der 16 ehemaligen Sowjetrepubliken.
Vorhergehende Doppelseite: Im silberglänzenden Vestibül sind alle Säulen mit spiegelnder Metallbeschichtung verkleidet.
Rechts: Seit der Auflösung der Sowjetunion sieht Russland die Aufgabe der Botschaften auch in der Vermittlung russischer Kultur. Im Konzertsaal mit 400 Plätzen finden deshalb oft Konzerte, Vorträge und Literaturveranstaltungen statt.
Unten: Unter der weißen Kuppel des Haupttreppenhauses prunken Materialien wie Marmor, Stuck, grüner Malachit und Goldbronze.

First page: the Great Hall, with capitals gleaming in gold leaf and the arms of the 16 former Soviet republics.
Previous pages: In the vestibule, resplendent in silver, all the pillars are faced with reflecting metal.
Right: Since the collapse of the Soviet Union, Russia has seen one task of its embassies as the mediation of Russian culture. The Concert Hall can seat 400 and is frequently used for concerts, talks and literature events.
Below: The main stairwell boasts splendour of marble, stucco, green malachite and golden bronze beneath a white cupola.

Première page: la salle héraldique avec ses chapiteaux dorés et les blasons des 16 ex-républiques soviétiques.
Double page précédente: L'argent brille de tous ses feux dans le vestibule où les colonnes sont habillées de métal miroitant.
A droite: Depuis la dissolution de l'Union soviétique, la Russie estime que ses ambassades doivent aussi faire connaître la culture russe. Des concerts, des conférences et des présentations littéraires ont donc souvent lieu dans la salle de concert de 400 places.
Ci-dessous: Sous la coupole blanche de la cage d'escalier principale, le marbre, le stuc, la malachite et le bronze doré étalent leur faste.

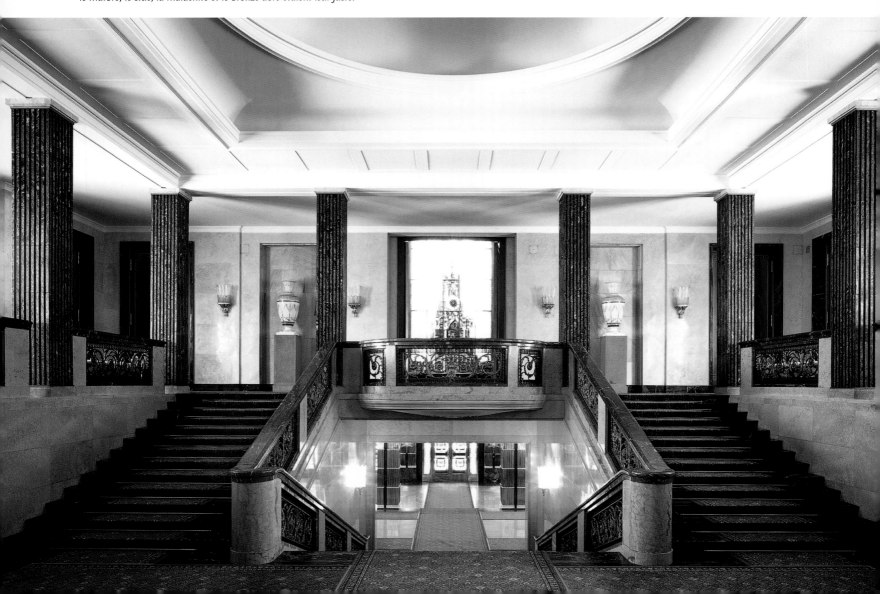

Oben: Im Spiegelsaal finden Empfänge, Verhandlungen und Konferenzen statt, wie beispielsweise 1954 die Außenministerkonferenz der vier Siegermächte.
Rechts: Der Jagdsalon hat zwei große, traditionelle Lackbilder mit Jagdszenen, die 1956 eigens für diesen Raum gemalt wurden.

Above: The hall of mirrors has seen receptions, negotiations and conferences, such as that held in 1954 by the foreign ministers of the four World War II Allies.
Right: The hunting room features two large, traditional lacquered paintings of hunting scenes, executed especially for this room in 1956.

Ci-dessus: Dans la Salle des miroirs ont lieu des réceptions, des négociations et des conférences, par exemple, en 1954, la conférence extraministérielle des quatre puissances victorieuses.
A droite: Le salon de chasse abrite deux grands tableaux de laque traditionnels, peints spécialement pour cette pièce en 1956.

Oben: In seiner Residenz empfängt Botschafter Sergey Krylov private Gäste.
Rechts: Blick vom Innenhof auf den Konzertsaal.
Rechte Seite: Der Damensalon mit den stoffbespannten Wänden wird als Empfangsraum für Gäste genutzt.

Above: Ambassador Sergei Krylov receives private guests in the ambassadorial residence.
Right: the concert hall seen from the courtyard.
Facing page: The ladies' salon with its walls covered with fine fabrics is used as a reception room for guests.

Ci-dessus: L'ambassadeur Sergeï Krylov reçoit des invités privés dans sa résidence.
A droite: la salle des concerts vue de la cour intérieure.
Page de droite: Les invités sont reçus dans le salon des dames aux murs tendus de tissu.

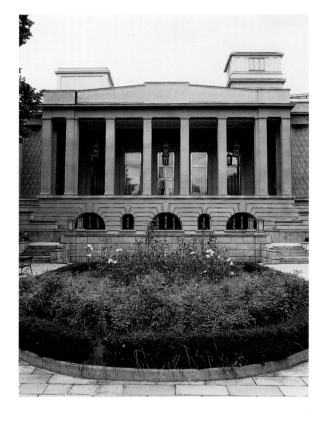

Anne Maria Jagdfeld designs interiors, creates fashion, develops projects, and manages the "Quartier 206 Departmentstore". Moreover, she has five sons and a family life that works. How does she do it all? Anne Maria Jagdfeld's secret is concentration. "I don't have time for a social life," she says. And she has good staff working with her. Since she and her husband are increasingly involved professionally with Berlin, they have set up in a downtown maisonette apartment. The living, cooking and dining areas are on the lower floor, the bedrooms, bathrooms and roof terrace upstairs. An oasis of tranquillity, with fabrics of warm colours, wood, and natural stone. After marrying, Jagdfeld studied art history, but she probably owes her expertise in art, materials and crafts to "a sound instinct, a trained eye and a cosmopolitan way of thinking". But she possesses more talents too, otherwise she would not be able to plan the interior of a luxury hotel on the Baltic and the new China Club in Berlin at the same time.

Anne Maria Jagdfeld

Anne Maria Jagdfeld ist Inneneinrichterin, Modedesignerin, Projektentwicklerin und Chefin des »Quartier 206 Departmentstore«. Außerdem hat sie fünf Söhne und ein funktionierendes Familienleben. Wie sie das schafft? Anne Maria Jagdfeld konzentriert sich. »Ich habe keine Zeit für Einladungen«, sagt sie. Und sie hat gute Mitarbeiter. Weil sie und ihr Mann immer mehr in Berlin zu tun haben, richteten sie sich mitten in der Stadt eine Maisonette-Wohnung ein. Unten Wohnen, Kochen, Essen, oben Schlafzimmer, Bäder und Dachterrassen. Eine Oase der Ruhe, mit Stoffen in warmen Farben, Hölzern und Naturstein. Jagdfeld studierte nach ihrer Hochzeit Kunstgeschichte, aber ihre Kenntnisse über Kunst, Materialien und Handwerk verdankt sie vermutlich »einfach einem guten Gespür, einem geschulten Auge und kosmopolitischem Denken«. Aber sie hat mehr Talente, denn sonst könnte sie nicht gleichzeitig das Interieur eines Grandhotels an der Ostsee und den neuen China-Club in Berlin planen.

Anne Maria Jagdfeld est styliste d'intérieur et de mode, conceptrice et dirige le «Quartier 206 Departmentstore». Elle a aussi cinq fils et une vie de famille satisfaisante. Comment fait-elle? «Je n'ai pas le temps pour les invitations», dit-elle après réflexion. Et elle a de bons collaborateurs. Se trouvant de plus en plus souvent à Berlin, elle et son mari se sont aménagé un appartement de plusieurs étages au centre de la ville. En bas séjour, cuisine, salle à manger, en haut chambres à coucher, salles de bains et terrasses sur le toit. Une oasis de sérénité avec des tissus chaleureux, du bois et de la pierre. Jagdfeld a étudié l'histoire de l'art, pourtant, selon elle, ses connaissances de l'art, des matériaux et de l'artisanat ne seraient que «du flair, un œil exercé et une pensée cosmopolite». Mais ses talents sont loin de se limiter à cela, sinon elle ne pourrait pas en même temps concevoir l'intérieur d'un hôtel sur la Baltique et le nouveau China Club de Berlin.

Vorhergehende Doppelseite: *perfekt abgestimmte Farben und Mate-rialien: blattvergoldete Glastüren, schwarzweißer Granitboden, ein schwarzer englischer Schiefertisch mit afrikanischer Maske, Venini-Vase und antiken japanischen Tempelleuchten.*
Rechts: *Blick vom Eingang durch goldene Türen ins Treppenhaus.*
Unten: *im Kaminzimmer zwei Kabinettschränke, entworfen von der Hausherrin. Sofa und Sessel sind eigens für das »Quartier 206 Departmentstore« hergestellt.*

Previous pages: *perfectly coordinated colours and materials: black and white granite flooring, a black English slate table with African mask, Venini vase and antique Japanese temple lanterns, glass doors with gold leaf.*
Right: *looking through the gold doors, from the entrance hall to the stairwell.*
Below: *The smokeroom features two cabinets designed by the lady of the house. The sofa and armchair were made especially for "Quartier 206 Departmentstore".*

Double page précédente: *des couleurs et des matériaux parfaitement harmonisés: sol de granit noir et blanc, une table anglaise noire en ardoise avec un masque africain, un vase de Venini et d'anciennes lanternes de temple japonaises, des portes en verre dorées à la feuille.*
A droite: *entre les portes dorées, la cage d'escalier vue de l'entrée.*
Ci-dessous: *dans le salon, près de la cheminée, deux armoires des-sinées par la maîtresse de maison. Le canapé et les fauteuils ont été spécialement fabriqués pour le «Quartier 206 Departmentstore».*

Oben: Den Esstisch hat die Hausherrin entworfen, die Stühle sind vom amerikanischen Designer J. Robert Scott. Fotos von Steven Klein aus der Jagdfeld-Sammlung und Arbeiten von Chris Ruhs.
Rechts: Aktzeichnungen aus Vietnam über dem Sofa im Schlafzimmer von Anne Maria Jagdfeld.

Above: The dining table was designed by the lady of the house, the chairs are by the American designer J. Robert Scott. Also shown are photos from the Jagdfeld collection by Steven Klein and works by Chris Ruhs.
Right: nude drawings from Vietnam over the sofa in Anne Maria Jagdfeld's bedroom.

Ci-dessus: La maîtresse de maison a dessiné la table, les chaises sont du designer américain J. Robert Scott. Photos de la collection Jagdfeld par Steven Klein et travaux de Chris Ruhs.
A droite: dessins de nus du Vietnam au-dessus du sofa dans la chambre à coucher d'Anne Maria Jagdfeld.

Oben: Im Schlafzimmer hängen Fotografien von Robert Mapplethorpe, Richard Avedon, Cecil Beaton und Horst P. Horst.
Rechts: Sorgfältig stimmt Anne Maria Jagdfeld Formen und Farben
aufeinander ab, egal ob es sich um Kunst- oder Gebrauchsgegenstände handelt.
Rechte Seite: raffinierte Strukturen: gehämmerter Lime Stone am
Boden, gerillter an der Wand. Die silbrig glänzende Wanne ist von
»Water Works« in London. Beim Baden schaut Patty Smith, foto-
grafiert von Steven Klein, zu.

Above: In the bedroom are photographs by Robert Mapplethorpe,
Richard Avedon, Cecil Beaton and Horst P. Horst.
Right: Anne Maria Jagdfeld carefully matches shapes with colours,
regardless if she deals with art or objects of daily use.
Facing page: The surfaces are sophisticated, with hammered limestone on the floor and fluted limestone on the walls. The gleaming
silvery tub is by "Water Works" of London. Looking on from a photograph by Steven Klein is Patty Smith.

Ci-dessus: dans la chambre à coucher, des photographies de Robert
Mapplethorpe, Richard Avedon, Cecil Beaton und Horst P. Horst.
A droite: Qu'il s'agisse d'œuvres d'art ou d'objets utilitaires, Anne
Maria Jagdfeld harmonise soigneusemment les formes et les couleurs.
Page de droite: limestone martelé sur le sol, rainé sur le mur. La
baignoire aux tons argentés est de «Water Works», Londres. Patty
Smith photographiée par Steven Klein regarde le baigneur.

Many a building in Berlin has a magnificent view, but there's none where you see the cathedral while you're swimming. None but Corinna Hoffmann's, that is – and she also built it herself. In 1998 she located her dream house, ready for conversion: 7,000 square metres of space, corridors 45 metres long with offices strung out along them, two inner courtyards and a dilapidated banqueting hall. "It was far too big," says Hoffmann, "and if I had known what I was letting myself in for, I wouldn't have bought it." The fact is that Corinna Hoffmann is a scholar of Romance languages and literatures, and apart from helping with a conversion she had no previous building experience. But now the house is finished, and she laughs as she tells of her difficulties. There are eight luxury lofts and five penthouse apartments in the building, a pool on the roof, and several terraces. The banqueting hall has been converted into a spa and lobby shared by all the residents. Corinna Hoffmann is pleased with her conversion, the fruits of which she can test every day in her own apartment.

Corinna Hoffmann

Es gibt viele Häuser mit grandioser Aussicht in Berlin, aber keines, auf dem man schwimmend den Dom im Auge hat. Hier wohnt Corinna Hoffmann und sie ist auch die Bauherrin. 1998 fand sie ihr Traumhaus zum Umbauen: 7000 Quadratmeter, 45 Meter lange Flure, an denen sich Büros reihten, zwei Innenhöfe und ein heruntergekommener Festsaal. »Es war viel zu groß«, sagt Hoffmann, »und wenn ich vorher gewusst hätte, was auf mich zukommt, hätte ich es nicht genommen.« Denn Corinna Hoffmann ist Romanistin und außer einer Assistenz bei einem Umbau hatte sie keine Bauerfahrung. Jetzt ist ihr Haus fertig und heute erzählt sie lachend von den Schwierigkeiten. Acht luxuriöse Lofts und fünf Penthousewohnungen hat das Haus, einen Pool auf dem Dach und mehrere Terrassen. Aus dem Festsaal wurde ein Spa und eine Lobby für alle Bewohner. Corinna Hoffmann ist zufrieden mit dem Umbau, den sie täglich in der eigenen Wohnung auf den Prüfstand stellt.

S'il existe à Berlin de nombreuses maisons offrant une vue grandiose, il n'y en a qu'une dans laquelle on peut contempler en nageant la cathédrale. C'est ici qu'habite Corinna Hoffmann, et elle en est aussi le maître d'œuvre. En 1998, elle trouva ce qui pouvait devenir la maison de ses rêves: 7000 mètres carrés, des corridors de 45 mètres de long où s'ouvraient des bureaux, deux cours intérieures et une salle des fêtes complètement délabrée. «Tout était beaucoup trop grand», dit Hoffmann «et si j'avais su ce qui m'attendait, je ne l'aurais pas pris». Il faut dire que Corinna Hoffmann est romaniste et qu'elle n'a aucune expérience de la construction. Aujourd'hui, elle peut rire des difficultés rencontrées. La maison abrite huit lofts luxueux et cinq penthouses, une piscine sur le toit et plusieurs terrasses. La salle des fêtes est devenue spa et lieu de réunion. Et Corinna Hoffmann peut tester jour après jour les transformations dans son propre appartement.

Seite 44/45: *fantastische Aussicht vom Dachgarten.*
Vorhergehende Doppelseite: *Das Spa mit 14-Meter-Pool, Goldsäulen und -tapete ist ein passender Rahmen für sportliche Auftritte.*
Linke Seite: *Eine Wand der sechs Meter hohen Gemeinschaftslobby ist mit einer geprägten Ornamenttapete beklebt.*
Oben: *vor dem Kamin im Wohnzimmer: ein Sofa von Zanotta und zwei Hocker aus DDR-Zeiten. Das Gemälde ist von Peter Halley.*
Rechts: *hinter dem langen Esstisch ein Sitzsack von Angela Bulloch.*

Pages 44/45: *a stupendous view from the roof terrace.*
Previous pages: *With its 14-metre pool and golden pillars and wallpaper, the spa is all round a superb place to keep in shape.*
Facing page: *One wall in the six-metre-high common lobby features a decorative embossed wallpaper.*
Above: *By the fireplace in the living room are a sofa by Zanotta and two hassocks dating from GDR times. The painting is by Peter Halley.*
Right: *In the corner beyond the long dining table is a pouffe by Angela Bulloch.*

Pages 44/45: *vue fantastique depuis le jardin suspendu.*
Double page précédente: *Le spa avec sa piscine de 14 mètres, ses colonnes et ses papiers peints dorés est un cadre adapté aux prouesses sportives.*
Page de gauche: *Un mur du foyer qui fait six mètres sous plafond est décoré de papier peint gaufré.*
Ci-dessus: *le séjour: face à la cheminée, un canapé de Zanotta et deux tabourets du temps de la RDA. Le tableau est signé Peter Halley.*
A droite: *derrière la longue table, un siège-sac d'Angela Bulloch.*

When he was four, what he most liked to do was pick flowers. His father was worried – until he started selling his bunches of flowers for 50 pfennigs a time. Frank Stüve became a florist. A star florist. Because he loves his profession, because he bears in mind who a bouquet is intended for, because he has his views, and is eager for knowledge, and is charming. And astoundingly hardworking. After a period of community service (in place of military service), Stüve worked on Norderney, in Brescia, in Krems and in Vienna. "In Italy I learned that flowers and passion go together," says Stüve. In Vienna he learned to speak the local dialect, because that way customers felt the advice they were given was better. And he met Gisela von Schenk. They resolved to open a store in Berlin together, specializing in flowers and interior design, and that was the start of "Villa Harteneck", which they have run since 1998. Frank Stüve's home is as meticulously arranged as one of his flower bouquets. "The settees mustn't have legs, otherwise the proportions of the space are ruined."

Frank Stüve

Als Vierjähriger pflückte er am liebsten Blumen. Vater Stüve sorgte sich um die Zukunft seines Sprösslings – bis dieser begann, die Sträuße für 50 Pfennig zu verkaufen. Frank Stüve wurde Florist. Ein Starflorist. Weil er seinen Beruf liebt, weil er weiß, für wen er welche Sträuße bindet, weil er eine Meinung hat, wissbegierig und charmant ist. Und wahnsinnig fleißig. Nach seinem Zivildienst arbeitete Stüve auf Norderney, in Brescia, in Krems und in Wien. »In Italien habe ich gelernt, dass Blumen und Leidenschaft zusammengehören«, sagt Stüve. In Wien lernte er wienerisch, weil die Kunden sich dann besser beraten fühlten. Und er traf Gisela von Schenk. Die beiden beschlossen, zusammen in Berlin ein Geschäft für Blumen und Interior zu eröffnen, und seit 1998 haben sie ihre »Villa Harteneck«. Genauso sorgfältig, wie er Blumen arrangiert, hat sich Stüve sein Zuhause eingerichtet. »Die Sofas dürfen keine Beine haben, sonst ist die Proportion des Raumes zerstört.«

A quatre ans, il adorait déjà cueillir des fleurs. Son père se fit du souci pour son avenir jusqu'à ce que Frank commence à vendre ses bouquets 50 pfennigs la pièce. Il est devenu fleuriste – et même une star. Parce qu'il aime son métier, qu'il sait quel bouquet offrir à telle personne, parce qu'il a ses idées à lui, qu'il est bourré de charme et curieux de tout. Et qu'il travaille comme un fou. A ses débuts, Stüve a travaillé à Norderney, à Brescia, à Krems et à Vienne. «En Italie, j'ai compris que les fleurs et la passion vont ensemble», dit-il. A Vienne, il a appris le viennois pour que ses clients se sentent mieux conseillés. Et puis il a rencontré Gisela von Schenk. Tous deux décidèrent alors d'ouvrir à Berlin un magasin réunissant les fleurs et les accessoires d'intérieur et, depuis 1998, ils ont leur «Villa Harteneck». Stüve a aménagé son domicile avec le même soin qu'il apporte à ses compositions florales. «Pas de pieds aux canapés, cela détruit les proportions de la pièce.»

Vorhergehende Doppelseite: Stüves Wohnung liegt in einem Innenhof – mitten in der Stadt und trotzdem ruhig. Frühstücksplatz am Fenster zum Hof.
Oben: Porträts von Wachsfiguren historischer Persönlichkeiten, die Hiroshi Sugimoto vor einem schwarzen Hintergrund fotografierte.
Rechts: Wohnraum mit zwei Verzelloni-Sesseln.
Rechte Seite: Blick vom Wohnraum in die Küche. Den Durchgang verengt eine von zwei Blumensäulen, die der Florist oft neu dekoriert.

Previous pages: Stüve's apartment faces onto an inner courtyard – in the heart of the city, but quiet nevertheless. The breakfast room is by a window onto the courtyard.
Above: portrait shots of wax models of historic personalities, photographed by Hiroshi Sugimoto against a black background.
Right: the living room, with two Verzelloni armchairs.
Facing page: looking from the living room towards the open-plan kitchen. The threshold is marked by one of two columns topped with floral displays which Stüve regularly changes.

Double page précédente: L'appartement de Stüve se trouve dans une cour intérieure – un îlot de paix au cœur de la ville. La table du petit déjeuner avec vue sur la cour.
Ci-dessus: Des figures de cire de personnages historiques, éclairées de manière dramatique et photographiées sur un fond noir par Hiroshi Sugimoto.
A droite: le séjour avec deux fauteuils Verzelloni.
Page de droite: la cuisine ouverte vue du séjour. L'entrée est marquée par l'une de deux colonnes florales que le fleuriste redécore souvent.

Rechts: *Die Küche schmücken vier ausgestopfte Fasane.*
Unten: *Stüve liebt klare Formen und Farben wie bei den Sofas von Ennio Verzelloni.*

Right: *Four stuffed pheasants hang decoratively in the kitchen.*
Below: *Stüve loves strong shapes and colours, as in Ennio Verzelloni's settees.*

A droite: *Quatre faisans empaillés décorent la cuisine.*
Ci-dessous: *Stüve aime les formes et les couleurs franches comme celles des canapés d'Ennio Verzelloni.*

Oben: *Die Sofatische sind einfache Blöcke aus Speckstein. Natürlich hat der Florist immer Blumenarrangements in seiner Wohnung.*
Rechts: *Über dem braunen Leder-Stahl-Bett des jungen deutschen Designers Philipp Plein liegt eine Kaninchenfelldecke. Die Fotos von Lord Snowdon zeigen die englische Gesellschaft bei einer Parade zu Ehren der Königin auf der Rennbahn.*

Above: *The coffee tables are simply blocks of soapstone. Naturally, Stüve the florist always has floral arrangements in his home.*
Right: *On the brown leather and steel by young German designer Philipp Plein is a rabbit fur counterpane. The photos by Lord Snowdon show English society at a parade in honour of the Queen and at the races.*

Ci-dessus: *Les tables sont de simples blocs de stéatite. Bien entendu, les compositions florales sont toujours présentes dans l'appartement.*
A droite: *Un dessus-de-lit en poils de lapin recouvre le lit cuir et acier conçu par le jeune designer allemand Philipp Plein. Les photos de Lord Snowdon montrent la société anglaise sur le champ de courses lors d'une parade en l'honneur de la reine.*

Felt has held a deep fascination for Christine Birkle ever since her student days when she discovered it. Back then she would full the wool for hours on end, trying out what this unconventional material was good for and what cuts suited it. Fortunately, the felt Birkle had taken such a shine to was just as useful for carpets or egg-warmers as for garments. At first she designed hats, which the Belgian Dries van Noten promptly had his models wear. Nowadays Birkle wraps up in felt jackets of her own creation, tailors dresses and skirts from a fabric of chiffon and felt, reclines in her Berlin apartment on felt cushions and quilts, and is delighted to find that the colour of her felt wall "puts me in a good mood every morning". Every year she designs two fashion and one home collection. She doesn't find it tedious to be limited to a single material. "Felt is unpredictable, every design is a fresh challenge." She gets her ideas anywhere and everywhere, even in the kitchen – "even a fried egg can be inspiring," declares Birkle.

Christine Birkle

Dem Filz ist Christine Birkle seit ihrem Studium verfallen. Damals entdeckte sie das Filzen, walkte stundenlang Wolle und probierte aus, für was und welche Schnitte sich das eigenwillige Material überhaupt eignet. Glücklicherweise taugt Birkles Filz genauso für Teppiche oder Eierwärmer wie für Kleidung. Zuerst entwarf sie Hüte, die der Belgier Dries van Noten sofort seinen Models auf den Kopf setzte. Jetzt wickelt sich Birkle in eigene Filzjacken, schneidert Kleider und Röcke aus einem Chiffon-Filz-Gespinst, sitzt in ihrer Berliner Wohnung auf Filzkissen und -decken und freut sich, weil die Farbe ihrer Filzwand »jeden Morgen gute Laune macht«. Eine Home- und zwei Modekollektionen entwirft sie jedes Jahr. Langweilig findet sie die Beschränkung auf ein einziges Material nicht. »Filz ist unberechenbar, jeder Entwurf ist eine neue Herausforderung.« Objektideen hat sie überall, selbst in ihrer Küche. Denn »auch ein Spiegelei kann mich inspirieren«, sagt Birkle.

Christine Birkle est tombée amoureuse du feutre quand elle était étudiante. Elle feutrait alors de la laine pendant des heures et étudiait les possibilités de ce matériau original. Heureusement, le feutre de Birkle peut aussi bien être transformé en tapis et en réchauffe-coquetiers qu'en vêtements. Elle a d'abord créé des chapeaux dont le Belge Dries Van Noten coiffa immédiatement ses mannequins. Aujourd'hui, Birkle porte ses propres vestes de feutre, taille des robes et des jupes dans un tissu de voile et de feutre, est assise chez elle sur des coussins et des couvertures de feutre et se réjouit de constater que la couleur de son mur de feutre la «met de bonne humeur tous les matins». Elle crée chaque année deux collections de vêtements et une collection de linge de maison. Elle ne s'en lasse pas. «Le feutre est déroutant, chaque projet est un nouveau défi.» Les idées lui viennent partout, même dans sa cuisine, car «même un œuf sur le plat peut m'inspirer», dit Birkle.

Linke Seite: Auf dem einfachen IKEA-Schrank, den Birkle mit Streifenfilz bezogen hat, stehen zwei von 20 Hutschachteln, die ihr Vater ihr zur Ladeneröffnung aus Spanholz geschreinert hat.
Oben und rechts: In der Küche hängen zwei gelbe Paneels aus Filz wie Felle an der Wand. Natürlich sind auch die zipfligen bunten Eier-wärmer und das Kleid aus Filz.
Folgende Doppelseite: Christine Birkle arbeitet auch zu Hause, um-geben von ihren Lieblingshausschuhen, Stoff- und Farbproben und gerade fertig gewordenen Kleidern.

Facing page: Atop the unprepossessing IKEA wardrobe, which Birkle has faced with strips of felt, are two of 20 plywood hat-boxes which her father made for her when the store opened.
Above and right: In the kitchen, two yellow panels of felt hang on the wall, like animal skins. Naturally the colourful egg-warmers and the dress are also felt.
Following pages: Christine Birkle works at home, amid her slippers, samples of fabrics and colours, and garments she has just completed.

Page de gauche: Birkle a habillé de feutre rayé une armoire d'IKEA sur laquelle trônent deux des 20 boîtes à chapeaux que son père a confectionnées pour elle quand elle a ouvert son magasin.
Ci-dessus et à droite: Dans la cuisine, deux panneaux de feutre jaune sont suspendus comme des peaux de bête. Les réchauffe-coquetiers pointus et colorés et la robe sont en feutre, cela va de soi.
Double page suivante: Christine Birkle travaille aussi chez elle, entourée de ses pantoufles préférées, d'échantillons de tissus et de couleurs et de vêtements qu'elle vient juste de terminer.

Oben: Für ihre Home Collection – Kissen, Teppiche, Decken – liebt Christine Birkle kräftige Farben.

Rechts: Für ein Hamburger Hotel entwarf Birkle Wandbespannungen, die sie in ihrem Schlafzimmer ausprobierte. Die knallrote Lampe hat sie wegen der Farbe ausgesucht.

Rechte Seite: Die Filzdecke auf dem Bett ist die größte Arbeit, die Birkle je hergestellt hat, denn es ist unheimlich aufwendig, ein drei Quadratmeter großes Stück im Wasser zu walken und danach zu trocknen.

Above: For her home collection – cushions, carpets, bedspreads – Christine Birkle loves strong colours.

Right: Birkle designed wall textiles for a Hamburg hotel and first tried them out in her own bedroom. She chose the bright red lamp for the colour.

Facing page: The felt bedspread was the biggest item Birkle has ever crafted. Fulling a piece three square metres in size in water, and then drying it, is strenuous work.

Ci-dessus: Pour la Home Collection – coussins, tapis, plaids – Christine Birkle affectionne les couleurs vigoureuses.

A droite: Birkle a essayé dans sa chambre à coucher les tentures murales conçues pour un hôtel de Hambourg. Elle a choisi la lampe à cause de sa couleur rouge vif.

Page de droite: Le dessus-de-lit en feutre est la plus grande pièce réalisée par Birkle; feutrer puis sécher trois mètres carrés de laine représente en effet énormément de travail.

Stephan Landwehr was planning to study; that at least was his reason for moving to Berlin and matriculating at the Academy of Art. It was there that he first encountered artists – those of the "Neue Wilden" (New Fauves) group, for instance, who stood Landwehr beers at their local, the "Exil", and whom he assisted in the studio in return. "I was chronically broke in those days," Landwehr recalls, "and doing odd jobs for artists was exciting." He stretched canvases, discussed painting, re-hung pictures and made frames. The frames were so good that all of his painter friends ordered them from him, finding them pleasing to the eye and precisely constructed. Landwehr had learnt a lot about painting, and that included how it was presented. It was most convenient to try out ideas on works in his own holdings – for he had begun to collect art, ever since he got his first commissions. Nowadays, the pictures he himself buys may remain unframed for a long time; Landwehr is so much in demand as a frame-maker that he hardly has any time any more.

Stephan Landwehr

Eigentlich hätte er studieren sollen, dafür jedenfalls war Stephan Landwehr nach Berlin gekommen und hatte sich an der Kunsthochschule eingeschrieben. Dort lernte er erst einmal Künstler kennen. Die »Neuen Wilden« beispielsweise, die in ihrer Stammkneipe »Exil« Landwehrs Bier bezahlten und denen er im Gegenzug im Atelier half. »Ich war damals chronisch pleite«, sagt Landwehr, »und bei Künstlern zu jobben war spannend.« Seit seinen ersten Jobs hatte er zu sammeln begonnen. Außerdem zog er Leinwände auf, diskutierte über Malerei, hängte Bilder um und baute Rahmen. So gute Rahmen, dass jeder seiner Malerfreunde diese Rahmen bestellte. Weil sie schön und präzise gebaut waren und immer genau zu den Arbeiten passten. Heute bleiben seine neu gekauften Bilder am längsten ungerahmt, denn Zeit hat der gefragte Rahmenbauer kaum noch.

Il était venu faire des études à Berlin et s'était même inscrit aux Beaux-Arts. Et puis, il fit la connaissance d'artistes, les «Neue Wilde» par exemple, qui lui payaient une bière dans leur taverne attitrée, «Exil», et auxquels il venait donner un coup de main. «J'étais toujours à sec», se souvient Landwehr, «et travailler avec des artistes, c'était excitant». Il tendait des toiles, parlait de peinture, accrochait des tableaux et fabriquait des cadres. Si bien d'ailleurs que tous ses amis peintres lui en commandaient: beaux, ajustés avec précision et toujours parfaitement adaptés aux toiles auxquels ils étaient destinés. C'est que Landwehr avait aussi appris à présenter la peinture. Et puis, il peut faire des essais avec sa propre collection d'œuvres d'art, entreprise dès qu'il a commencé à travailler. Curieusement, les toiles achetées dernièrement ne sont pas encore encadrées car notre constructeur de cadres est si demandé qu'il n'a plus guère de temps à leur consacrer.

Vorhergehende Doppelseite: *Mitten im Loft steht eine funktions-fähige Toilette – Kunst der Britin Sarah Lucas. An der Wand Zeich-nungen von Raymond Petibon und eine Arbeit von John Miller. Das Gemälde rechts ist von Daniel Richter, darunter ein Foto von Angus Fairhurst. Über dem Eingang ein Siebdruck von Albert Oehlen.*
Rechts: *großes Schriftbild des Amerikaners Sean Landers, darunter Zeichnungen von John Bock.*
Unten: *Sofa und Sessel hat Landwehr selbst entworfen und gebaut, davor zwei Skulpturen von Manfred Pernice. Natürlich sind auch die weißen gestapelten Stühle eine Skulptur – von Maria Eichhorn.*

Previous pages: *Right in the middle of the loft is a working toilet – or rather, an artwork by British artist Sarah Lucas. On the wall is a photo that goes with it, drawings by Raymond Petibon and a work by John Miller. The painting on the right is by Daniel Richter, and below it a photo by Angus Fairhurst. Above the entrance is a silk-screen print by Albert Oehlen.*
Right: *large calligraphic artwork by the American Sean Landers, below it drawings by John Bock.*
Below: *settee and armchair designed and constructed by Landwehr himself. Near them are two sculptures by Manfred Pernice. Naturally the white stacked chairs are also a sculpture, by Maria Eichhorn.*

Double page précédente: *Au milieu du loft, un siège d'aisances par-faitement opérationnel – une œuvre de l'artiste britannique Sarah Lucas. Au mur, la photographie correspondante, des dessins de Ray-mond Petibon et un travail de John Miller. Le tableau à droite est signé Daniel Richter, en dessous une photo d'Ingus Fairhurst. Au-dessus de l'entrée, une sérigraphie d'Albert Oehlen.*
A droite: *un grand tableau de l'Américain Sean Landers, au-dessus de dessins de John Bock.*
Ci-dessous: *Landwehr a fabriqué lui-même le canapé et les fauteuils. Devant eux, deux sculptures de Manfred Pernice. Les chaises blanches empilées sont aussi une sculpture – de Maria Eichhorn.*

Oben: Landwehr ist ein fantastischer Gastgeber, besonders im Sommer wird auf seiner Hofterrasse gegrillt und ausdauernd gefeiert. An der langen Wand des Loft hängen drei große Bilder: von Sean Landers, Tal R und Peter Doig.
Rechts: Auch das Bett hat der Rahmenmacher selbst entworfen. Darüber ein Gemälde von Sean Landers.

Above: Landwehr is a celebrated host, and in the summer especially there are barbecues on his terrace and the parties run and run. On the long wall of the loft are three large pictures, by Sean Landers, Tal R and Peter Doig.
Right: The bed too was designed by Landwehr himself. Over it is a painting by Sean Landers.

Ci-dessus: Landwehr est un hôte fantastique. En été surtout, on fait la fête et des barbecues sur sa terrasse. Sur le long mur du loft, trois grands tableaux de Sean Landers, Tal R et Peter Doig.
A droite: Landwehr a également dessiné le lit que domine un tableau de Sean Landers.

There's no doubt about it, Jonathan Meese is an artist. For two years he has been making an international career with his performances, installations and paintings. Meese doesn't really take much of an interest in living spaces, despite the fact that he has three apartments – in Hamburg, in Ahrensburg at his mother's, and in Berlin. He describes himself as interested "in the period from the second day of Creation till 18,000 A.D." and for that reason he reads a great deal and collects everything, from newspaper clippings to plastic swords. "I have to have everything around me all the time," says Meese, "and if I feel like painting at three in the morning, I have to be able to do it right away, in my pyjamas if need be." Really he requires his apartment only as a storage space, a studio, and a private cinema for viewing his three favourite videos, "Zardoz", "Caligula" and "A Clockwork Orange" – and so that he can listen to music while he paints, preferably by DAF. He might just as well sleep at friends' places. And to brew a cup of tea you don't really need a whole kitchen.

Jonathan Meese

Kein Zweifel, Jonathan Meese ist Künstler. Einer, der seit zwei Jahren eine internationale Karriere mit Performances, Installationen und Gemälden macht. Fürs Wohnen interessiert sich Meese eigentlich nicht, obwohl er immerhin drei Wohnungen hat – in Hamburg, in Ahrensburg bei seiner Mutter und in Berlin. Weil er sich »für den Zeitraum vom zweiten Tag der Schöpfung bis 18 000 n. Chr.« interessiert, liest er viel und sammelt alles, vom Zeitungsausschnitt bis zum Plastikschwert. »Ich muss alles ständig um mich herum haben«, sagt Meese, »und wenn ich nachts um drei malen will, dann muss ich loslegen können, auch im Schlafanzug.« Eigentlich braucht er seine Wohnungen nur als Lager, als Atelier und als Heimkino für seine drei Lieblingsvideos »Zardoz«, »Caligula« und »Clockwork Orange« – und um beim Malen Musik zu hören, am liebsten die von DAF. Schlafen könne man ja auch bei Freunden und fürs Tee kochen brauche man ja nicht gleich eine ganze Küche.

Jonathan Meese est un créateur, c'est sûr. Depuis deux ans, il poursuit une carrière internationale avec des performances, des installations et des peintures. A vrai dire, bien qu'il ait trois appartements – à Hambourg, à Ahrensburg chez sa mère, et à Berlin –, il n'a aucun goût pour son intérieur. Comme il s'intéresse à l'époque qui va «du deuxième jour de la Création à 18 000 après Jésus-Christ», il lit beaucoup et collectionne tout, de l'article de journal à l'épée en plastique. «Je dois avoir tout sans cesse autour de moi», dit Meese, «et si je veux peindre à trois heures du matin, je dois pouvoir m'y mettre, même en pyjama.» En fait ses appartements ne lui servent que de dépôt, d'atelier et de salle privée pour regarder ses trois vidéos favorites «Zardoz», «Caligula» et «L'Orange mécanique» et aussi pour écouter de la musique en peignant, en particulier celle de DAF. Après tout, on peut toujours dormir chez des amis et nul besoin de cuisine équipée pour se faire un tasse de thé.

ICH HABE EINEN TRAUM

David Lynch, 53, ...

»Es ist ein bewölkter Tag, ein Schwarzweißtag. Etwas von einem Wind ist zu spüren, und von fern, gedämpft kommt der Beat von Reggae-Dub. Es ist kein fröhlicher Reggae.«

KULTUR

Rechts vor links

Wände Foto-Abenteuer aus der Luft

Cool designer apartments equipped for hosting dinner parties are not to the taste of photographer and film-maker Ralf Schmerberg. He would rather have something more unconventional. And in that preference he has his principles. "The apartment has to have a floor you can make a mess on. And you have to be able to shift the furniture quickly." He has his reasons. He has moved 20 times – and the parties he throws in his flat are legendary. At times, he and the lady who shares the apartment have fun on their own – letting off their fireworks ahead of New Year's Eve, or tipping out tons of confetti when the "Fuck Parade" was passing. The memory still makes him laugh. But Schmerberg's apartment isn't only for fun. In his studio he created his new film "Poems" and conceived his successful advertising spots. This too, though, seems to be fun for him rather than stressful work.

Ralf Schmerberg

Kühle Designerwohnungen, wo man »Dinnerchen« macht, liegen dem Fotografen und Filmemacher Ralf Schmerberg nicht. Er mag lieber das Unkonventionelle. Und dafür hat er Prinzipien. »Die Wohnung muss immer einen Boden haben, auf dem man kleckern kann. Und die Einrichtung muss man schnell umrücken können.« Der Mann weiß warum. 20 Mal ist er umgezogen und die Partys in seiner Wohnung sind Legende. Manchmal amüsieren er und seine Mitbewohnerin sich aber auch allein. Wenn sie Knaller und Raketen schon vor Silvester auf die Straße schossen oder tonnenweise Konfetti auf die vorbeiziehende »Fuck-Parade« kippten. Darüber lacht er heute noch. Aber Schmerberg hat seine Wohnung nicht nur zum Amüsieren. Im Atelier hat er seinen neuen Film »Poems« erarbeitet und seine erfolgreichen Werbefilme konzipiert. Aber auch das scheint ihm keinen Stress, sondern Spaß zu bringen.

Les froids appartements de designers où l'on fait la «dînette» ne sont pas l'affaire de Ralf Schmerberg, photographe et cinéaste. Il préfère ce qui n'est pas conventionnel et il a des idées bien arrêtées. «On doit pouvoir faire des taches par terre et déplacer les meubles rapidement.» Il sait de quoi il parle, vu qu'il a déjà déménagé 20 fois et que ses fêtes sont mythiques. Ce n'est pas que lui et celle qui partage son appartement ne sont pas capables de se distraire seuls – il rit encore en repensant au jour où ils ont fait éclater des pétards et des fusées dans la rue avant la Saint-Sylvestre, ou jeté des tonnes de confetti sur la «fuck-parade» qui passait. Mais Schmerberg ne fait pas que s'amuser dans son appartement. Il a élaboré dans son atelier son nouveau film «Poems» et y a conçu ses films publicitaires réussis. Pourtant, ici non plus pas de stress visible, mais du plaisir.

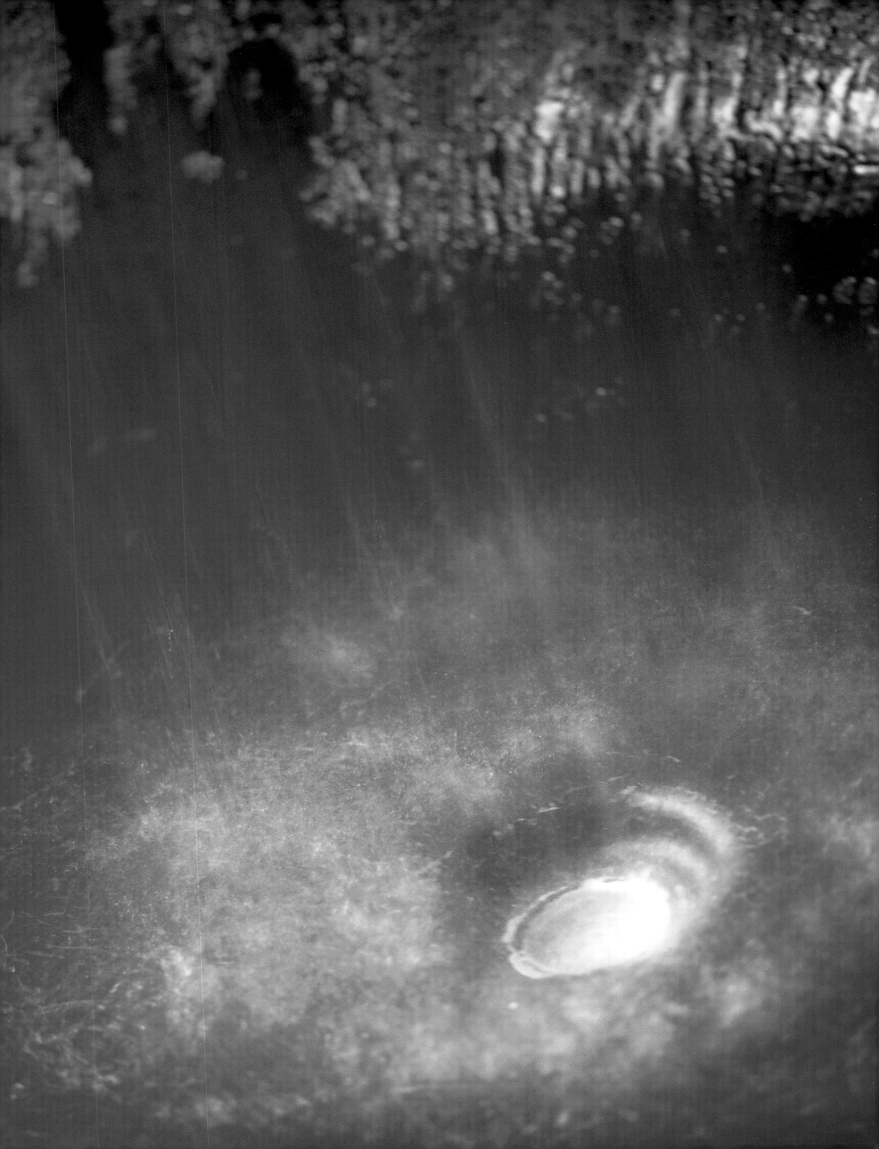

Laura Kikauka is an artist, even if she prefers to be describe as a professional maker of found craftworks. She also describes herself as a "collectoholic". "But I don't go looking for things," Kikauka insists – "they find me." In her "Funny Farm East" there's still room for witty, kitschy, weird and wonderful garbage of the kind an affluent society generates, especially at times when parts of the Gesamtkunstwerk that is her flat happen to be on display in a museum. At those times she finds her home rather empty. Laura Kikauka lives in her cluttered "Funny Farm East", which serves her as art studio, sound studio, depository and artwork all in one. It is in the last moribund crumbling house on Hackescher Markt, an address which has seen high-grade stylish renovation all round, and there she works on her finds, bringing the junk to life with a few simple electronic tricks, constructing miniature motors, soldering, gluing and welding. Chaos isn't something she goes for, says Kikauka: everything in her apartment is arranged according to colour, material, shape and size.

Laura Kikauka

Laura Kikauka ist Künstlerin, auch wenn ihr die Bezeichnung »Profibastlerin« lieber ist. Und nach eigenen Angaben ist sie »collectoholic«, süchtige Sammlerin. »Allerdings suche ich keine Dinge«, behauptet Kikauka, »sondern die Sachen finden mich.« Für witzigen, kitschigen, kuriosen Wohlstandsmüll ist immer noch Platz in ihrer »Funny Farm East«, besonders, wenn Teile ihres »Gesamtkunstwerks Wohnung« gerade in einem Museum gezeigt werden. Dann findet sie es leer bei sich zu Hause. Laura Kikauka lebt in ihrer zugewucherten »Funny Farm East«, die gleichzeitig ihr Atelier, ihre Werkstatt, ihr Tonstudio, ihr Lager und ein Kunstwerk ist. Im letzten morbide bröckelnden Haus am nobel renovierten Hackeschen Markt bastelt sie an ihren Fundstücken, bringt den Trödel mit ein paar einfachen elektronischen Tricks zum Leben, baut Minimotoren, lötet, klebt und schweißt. Chaos möge sie nicht, sagt Kikauka, bei ihr sei alles nach Farbe, Material, Form, Größe geordnet.

Laura Kikauka est une artiste, même si elle préfère le terme «bricoleuse professionnelle». Elle est aussi une collectionneuse acharnée et ne s'en cache pas. «A ceci près que je ne cherche pas les choses, ce sont elles qui me trouvent». Il y a toujours de la place dans sa «Funny Farm East» pour les déchets marrants, kitsch, bizarres de la société de consommation – surtout en ce moment, vu que des parties de son «Œuvre d'art totale Appartement» sont exposées dans un musée. C'est bien vide chez elle, trouve-t-elle, dans le dernier bâtiment qui s'effrite de manière morbide sur la Hackesche Platz noblement rénovée. Dans cette maison cachée sous les objets et qui est à la fois son atelier, son studio d'enregistrement, son dépôt et une œuvre d'art, elle vit, bricole, anime ses trouvailles avec quelques trucs électroniques simples, construit des moteurs miniatures, soude et colle. Kikauka dit ne pas aimer le chaos – chez elle tout est rangé par couleur, matériau, forme et taille.

Seite 112/113: *Der Weg zum Atelierhaus führt durch mehrere Höfe.*
Vorhergehende Doppelseite: *Wohnraum und Atelier.*
Oben: *»Liebesgrotte« nennt Kikauka ihr rundes Bett mit elektrischem Massagekissen und Raubtierdruck-Decken.*
Rechts: *Perückenlager, Schminkplatz, Garderobe, Archiv.*
Rechte Seite: *Eigentlich ist Kikauka eine begeisterte Köchin, hier kocht sie allerdings fast nur Teewasser. Aber ihren Kühlschrank benutzt sie oft – weil er beim Öffnen Musik macht.*

Pages 112/113: *The way to the studio building passes through a number of courtyards.*
Previous pages: *living space and studio.*
Above: *Kikauka calls her rounded bed her "love grotto". It has electric massage cushions and the counterpanes are printed to resemble the fells of beasts of prey.*
Right: *wig store, make-up room, wardrobe, archive.*
Facing page: *Kikauka loves cooking, but here she fixes little beyond a cup of tea. She is a regular with the fridge, though – because it plays music when she opens it.*

Pages 112/113: *Il faut traverser plusieurs cours pour arriver à l'atelier*
Double page précédente: *séjour et atelier.*
Ci-dessus: *La «grotte d'amour» de Kikaula: un lit rond avec coussin de massage électrique et dessus-de-lit façon félin.*
A droite: *dépôt de perruques, cabinet de maquillage, archives.*
Page de droite: *Kikauka adore faire la cuisine, mais ici elle se contente de faire bouillir l'eau du thé. Néanmoins, elle utilise souvent son réfrigérateur parce qu'il fait de la musique quand elle l'ouvre.*

Berlin Interiors   Laura Kikauka

Kreuzberg & Friedrichshain

He needs the Paris Bar as a stage, he needs the regulars, the audience, but Michel Würthle also needs to be able to retreat to his apartment in an old building in Kreuzberg. There he writes, draws and paints. "A solitary and sometimes painful process of sublimation," as Würthle once described art. At that time he was known not so much as an artist, but rather as a practitioner of the art of life, the landlord of the Paris Bar, welcoming in his guests with an air now charming, now ironic, now cynical. Always knowing that art is about life. The right life, the life that is dreamed of, perhaps in vain. Würthle knows this from his profound and never-ending conversations with artist friends such as Martin Kippenberger. It was Kippenberger who encouraged Würthle, who had studied art, to return to practising it. And since 1994 the boss of the Paris Bar has been exhibiting his drawings – the observations and insights of a psychologist fast on the draw, of a bar owner recording what he knows once he is off the Paris Bar stage.

Michel Würthle

Er braucht die Paris Bar als Bühne, er braucht die Gäste, das Publikum, aber Michel Würthle braucht auch den Rückzug in seine Kreuzberger Altbauwohnung. Dort schreibt, zeichnet und malt er. »Eine einsame und manchmal schmerzvolle Arbeit der Sublimation«, hat Würthle einmal über Kunst gesagt. Damals kannte man ihn, den Künstler, vielleicht nur als Lebenskünstler, als den Wirt der Paris Bar, der die Gäste begrüßt, mal charmant, mal ironisch, manchmal zynisch. Mit dem Wissen, dass es nur in der Kunst um Leben geht. Um das richtige, das vergebliche, das erträumte Leben. Würthle weiß das, weil er die tiefsten und endlosesten Gespräche mit seinen Künstlerfreunden geführt hat. Mit Martin Kippenberger beispielsweise. Der ermutigte den ehemaligen Kunststudenten Würthle, wieder als Künstler zu arbeiten. Seit 1994 stellt der Chef der Paris Bar seine Zeichnungen aus – Beobachtungen und Erkenntnisse eines »Schnellpsychologen« und Wirts.

Il a besoin de la scène du Paris Bar, de ses clients, de la présence du public, mais Michel Würthle a aussi besoin de se retirer dans son appartement ancien à Kreuzberg. Ici, il écrit, dessine et peint. «Un travail de sublimation, solitaire et parfois douloureux», a-t-il dit un jour, parlant de l'art. A l'époque on ne le connaissait, lui le créateur, que comme le tenancier du Paris Bar, celui qui salue les clients, parfois charmant, parfois ironique, quelquefois cynique, tout en sachant que seul l'art traite vraiment de la vie. De la vraie vie, la vie vaine, la vie rêvée. Würthle a appris cela au cours de ses conversations les plus profondes et les plus interminables avec ses amis artistes, Martin Kippenberger, par exemple. C'est lui qui a encouragé l'ex-étudiant des beaux-arts à se remettre au travail. Depuis 1994, le chef du Paris Bar expose ses dessins – observations et découvertes d'un «psychologue de comptoir», qu'il fixe sur le papier quand il quitte la scène du Paris Bar.

*Vorhergehende Doppelseite: An allen Wänden von Würthles Altbau-
wohnung hängen Bilder von Freunden und von ihm selbst.*
*Oben: der Hausherr an seinem Arbeitstisch vor einer Bilderwand. In
der Mitte ein Gemeinschaftsgemälde von ihm und Damien Hirst.*
*Rechts: Zeichnungen der Berlinerin Ina Barfuss von 1981, davor
afrikanische Skulpturen.*
*Rechte Seite: Neben der Tür ein Gemälde des Kongolesen Moké, ein
Porträt, das Catherine Würthle 1996 von ihrem Mann gemacht hat,
und bemalte Holzskulpturen von Michel Würthle.*

*Previous pages: The walls in Würthle's classic old apartment are
covered with pictures by friends and by himself.*
*Above: Würthle at his desk, before a wall of pictures. The painting in
the middle was a collaborative work with Damien Hirst.*
*Right: drawings by Berlin artist Ina Barfuss, dating from 1981, with
African sculptures in the foreground.*
*Facing page: Beside the door are a painting by the Congo artist
Moké, a portrait Catherine Würthle painted of her husband in 1996
and wooden sculptures by Michel Würthle.*

Double page précédente: les dessins de ses amis et les siens.
*Ci-dessus: le maître de maison à son bureau. Au mur, un grand
tableau réalisé en commun avec Damien Hirst.*
*A droite: derrière des statuettes africaines, des dessins réalisés en 1981
par la Berlinoise Ina Barfuss.*
*Page de droite: Près de la porte, un tableau du Congolais Moké, un
portrait de Michel Würthle peint par sa femme Catherine en 1996 et
des bois sculptés peints par le maître de maison.*

Rechts und unten: *Wenn keine Bilder an den Wänden hängen, dann stehen dort Bücherregale. Würthle liest nicht nur viel, er schreibt auch. Auf der Fensterbank hinter dem Arbeitstisch stehen Werke von Würthles Künstlerfreunden Günther Brus und Martin Kippenberger.*

Right and below: *Wherever there are no pictures on the walls, there are bookshelves. Würthle not only reads a great deal, he also writes. On the window sill behind the desk are works by his artist friends Günther Brus and Martin Kippenberger.*

A droite et ci-dessous: *Là où il n'y a pas de tableaux, il y a des bibliothèques. Non seulement Würthle lit beaucoup mais il écrit. Sur l'appui de fenêtre, derrière le bureau, des œuvres de Günther Brus et Martin Kippenberger, des amis de Würthle.*

Oben: Den Sportgeräten verdankt der Wirt der Paris Bar nicht nur seine gute Figur, sondern auch die Kondition für durchfeierte Nächte.
Rechts: über dem Bett eine Serie von Zeichnungen des Künstlers Werner Büttner.

Above: If he didn't do something to keep fit, the landlord of the Paris Bar would neither keep his figure nor be able to cope with all-night carousing.
Right: Over the bed is a set of drawings by Werner Büttner.

Ci-dessus: Les appareils de musculation ont donné au tenancier du Paris Bar un belle silhouette mais aussi le tonus nécessaire à la vie de noctambule.
A droite: au-dessus du lit, une série de dessins de Werner Büttner.

Andreas Hierholzer really wanted to live and work in Los Angeles. After completing a German diploma in architecture, he took his master's degree in L.A. and found himself a job. But then the Wall came down. There was no question that Hierholzer, a Berliner by birth, would return to Berlin right away. Friends helped him find his apartment: three rooms, eighty-five square metres in all, in a central but quiet location, with new heating, bare plastered walls and a tenancy agreement that bound him not to overpaint the ceiling paintings. In the process of renovation Hierholzer fell well and truly in love with his new home, for nearly every detail was still original. The date when the house was built is on the wall, on a scrap of newspaper from 1895 stuck to it. In the 19th century, newsprint was used as an additional insulating layer under wallpaper. Hierholzer hasn't regretted moving back to Berlin: in the meantime his office has built a factory, a residential development and the Embassy of Oman.

Andreas Hierholzer

Eigentlich wollte Andreas Hierholzer in Los Angeles leben und arbeiten. Dort hatte er nach seinem deutschen Architekturdiplom den Master gemacht und gerade einen Job gefunden. Doch dann fiel die Mauer. Klar, dass Hierholzer, gebürtiger Berliner, sofort nach Berlin ging. Seine Wohnung fand er damals durch Freunde: drei Zimmer, 85 Quadratmeter, zentral und ruhig gelegen, neue Heizung, blanker Putz und ein Mietvertrag, in dem er sich verpflichtete, die Deckengemälde nicht zu übermalen. Beim Renovieren verliebte sich Hierholzer regelrecht in sein neues Zuhause, denn fast alle Details waren noch im Originalzustand. Das Baujahr des Hauses hat Hierholzer schriftlich: An der Wand klebt bis heute eine Zeitung von 1895. Damals diente sie als Makulatur unter der Tape-te. Seine Entscheidung für Berlin hat Hierholzer nicht bereut: Sein Büro hat inzwischen eine Fabrik, eine Wohnsiedlung und die Botschaft des Oman gebaut.

A vrai dire, c'est à Los Angeles qu'Andreas Hierholzer voulait vivre et travailler. Il y avait d'ailleurs obtenu le master après son diplôme allemand d'architecte et venait de trouver un travail. Et puis le mur de Berlin est tombé. Hierholzer est retourné aussitôt dans la ville où il est né, et ses amis lui ont trouvé un appartement: trois pièces, 85 mètres carrés, situé au centre et calme, nouveau chauffage, murs non tapissés et un contrat de location dans lequel il s'engage à ne pas recouvrir les peintures du plafond. Pendant les travaux, Hierholzer est tombé amoureux de son nouveau foyer, car presque tous les détails étaient restés dans leur état d'origine. La date de construction de la maison est inscrite noir sur blanc: un journal est resté collé au mur sous les papiers peints depuis 1895. Hierholzer n'a jamais regretté sa décision de s'établir à Berlin: son agence a entre-temps construit une usine, un lotissement d'habitations et l'ambassade d'Oman.

Matthias Roeingh, alias Dr. Motte, is the man who had the idea for Berlin's Love Parade. Together with his partner, designer Heike Mühlhaus, Dr. Motte lives right at the top. Out of sight of everyone, because their penthouse is atop a building with a listed façade. What's more, this being so, they have a wall right in front of their noses on one side of the flat. But it doesn't bother them. "It's a pink object with a lot of advantages," Mühlhaus declares: "when I wake up, my thoughts turn to Miami right away." For Dr. Motte, this Miami is rather a drawback, though. On sunny days the pink reflects the light so powerfully that at times he cannot make out the light signals on the sound-effects machines, delays, mixing desks and keyboards in his doubly-soundproofed studio. Mühlhaus designed the interior in its entirety, from kitchen to fireplace. Only the cast concrete wash-basins were Dr. Motte's; before he evolved into Germany's best-known DJ he worked as a concrete pourer.

Dr. Motte & Heike Mühlhaus

Matthias Roeingh alias Dr. Motte ist der Erfinder der Berliner Love-Parade. Mit seiner Lebensgefährtin, der Designerin Heike Mühlhaus, lebt Dr. Motte ganz oben. Unsichtbar, denn ihr Penthouse steht auf einem Gebäude mit denkmalgeschützter Fassade. Deshalb haben die beiden auf einer Seite ihrer Wohnung eine mannshohe Wand vor der Nase. Macht aber nichts. »Ein pinkfarbenes Objekt mit vielen Vorteilen«, nennt Mühlhaus die Mauer, »wenn man aufwacht, denkt man gleich an Miami.« Für Dr. Motte ist dieses Miami eher von Nachteil. An Sonnentagen reflektiert die rosa Farbe das Licht so stark, dass er manchmal in seinem Studio die Lichtsignale an den Effektgeräten, Delays, Mischpulten und Keyboards nicht erkennen kann. Mühlhaus hat die Innenarchitektur entworfen, von der Küche bis zum Kamin. Nur die Waschbecken aus Beton sind von Dr. Motte, denn bevor er der bekannteste DJ Deutschlands wurde, hatte er als Betonbauer gearbeitet.

Matthias Roeingh alias Dr Motte est l'inventeur de la Love Parade. Avec sa compagne, la styliste Heike Mühlhaus, il vit haut perché. Leur penthouse est invisible car il se trouve sur un bâtiment dont la façade est protégée, ce qui explique pourquoi le couple a un mur haut comme un homme sous les yeux sur tout un côté de l'appartement. Aucune importance. «Un objet rose avec beaucoup d'avantages», trouve Mühlhaus, «au réveil, je pense tout de suite à Miami.» Ce Miami-là, le Dr Motte, lui, s'en passerait bien. En effet, quand le soleil brille, la paroi rose bonbon reflète si fort la lumière que dans son studio à double isolation phonique il ne reconnaît plus les signaux lumineux de ses appareils d'effet, delays, tables de mixage et claviers. La décoration intérieure est l'œuvre de Heike Mühlhaus, de la cuisine à la cheminée. Seuls les éviers en béton sont signés Motte qui a travaillé comme bétonneur avant de devenir le DJ le plus connu d'Allemagne.

Until artist Erik Schmidt rented his studio flat, he knew nothing about former East Germany's massive prefab blocks, and United Nations Square was an address that had no connotations for him. Schmidt, needless to say, is a "Wessi". Every citizen of the GDR was familiar with the "snake" and the "boomerang", developments totalling 1,280 apartments in the heart of the city, built in 1968 by Hermann Henselmann. In those days, only East Germans who toed the Party line were allowed to move into these flats; now it is Schmidt who is privileged, not because of his political views but because in the entire block there are only six flats of the type he wanted, with a studio and roof garden. His new home has even influenced his art: he has painted the view from the window, made a video, and devised a fictional home story as an art project. He sent photos from this project to advertising agencies – the dreary concrete legacy of Socialist architecture happens to be hip at present, so Schmidt's apartment is often used as a backdrop for TV ads or pop videos.

Erik Schmidt

Bevor der Künstler Erik Schmidt seine 130 Quadratmeter große Atelierwohnung mietete, wusste er nichts über Plattenbauten, und der Platz der Vereinten Nationen war für ihn Niemandsland. Natürlich ist Schmidt »Wessi«, denn jeder DDR-Bürger kannte die »Schlange« und den »Bumerang« mit 1280 Wohnungen mitten in der Stadt, 1968 gebaut vom sozialistischen Chefarchitekten Hermann Henselmann. Damals durften dort nur linientreue DDR-Bürger einziehen, heute ist Schmidt privilegiert. Nicht wegen seiner Gesinnung, sondern weil es seinen Wohnungstyp mit Atelier und Dachgarten nur sechs Mal in dem Block gibt. Das neue Zuhause hat sogar seine Kunst beeinflusst: Er malte den Blick aus seinem Fenster, drehte ein Video und dachte sich als Kunstprojekt eine fiktive Homestory aus. Davon schickte er Fotos an Werbeagenturen. Und weil die sozialistische Betontristesse gerade hip ist, dient Schmidts Wohnung oft als Kulisse für Werbespots oder Pop-Videos.

Avant de louer son atelier de 130 mètres carrés, le créateur Erik Schmidt ne savait rien des cités ni de la Place des Nations-Unies. Forcément, c'est un «Wessi», un Allemand de l'Ouest. Les citoyens de l'Est, eux, connaissaient le «Serpent» et le «Boomerang», construits en 1968 par le chef architecte socialiste Hermann Henselmann. A l'époque, ces 1280 appartements du centre-ville étaient réservés à ceux qui étaient fidèles à la ligne politique du parti. Aujourd'hui Schmidt est un privilégié, pas à cause de ses idées mais parce que le type d'appartement qu'il habite, avec atelier et jardin suspendu, n'existe que six fois dans le bloc. Son nouveau logis a même influencé son art: il a peint ce qu'il voit de sa fenêtre, tourné un film vidéo et imaginé une homestory destinée à un projet artistique. Il en a envoyé des photos à des agences de publicité. Et comme le béton triste est hype en ce moment, son appartement sert souvent de décor à des spots publicitaires et des vidéos pop.

Linke Seite und oben: Als Schmidt die Tapeten abnahm, kam der blanke Plattenbeton hervor, den er in einigen Räumen so beließ, woanders kleben als Reminiszenz die alten Muster noch an der Wand wie Bilder.
Rechts: Viele Möbel stammen aus der ehemaligen DDR, andere sind vom Trödel. Der Tisch von IKEA passt zu allem.
Folgende Doppelseite: Wendeltreppe zum Dachatelier; Details aus Küche, Atelier, Wohn- und Schlafraum.

Facing page and above: When Schmidt stripped the wallpaper he was left with bare concrete. In some rooms he preserved the walls in their raw state, in others he left samples of wallpaper, like pictures, as a kind of souvenir.
Right: Much of the furniture dates from old East German times, much else is from junk sales. The IKEA table goes with anything.
Following pages: spiral staircase to the rooftop studio: details of the kitchen, studio, living room and bedroom.

Page de gauche et ci-dessus: Sous les papiers peints, il n'y avait que le béton nu. Dans quelques pièces, Schmidt a laissé les murs tels quels, dans d'autres les vieux motifs sont restés collés au mur comme des tableaux-souvenirs.
A droite: De nombreux meubles viennent de l'ex-RDA, d'autres de la brocante. La table d'IKEA va avec tout.
Double page suivante: Un escalier en colimaçon mène à l'atelier; détails de la cuisine, de l'atelier, du séjour et de la chambre à coucher.

Morgane and Emma divide their time between a number of homes:
a small apartment in Paris, the loveliest in Berlin, and also one in
Miami. The last is their original home, if a sanctuary for stray animals
merits the name. Fortunately, their master took them away from the
place. First he took Morgane, and later he came back, with his lady
friend, having realised that everything is much more fun when there's
two of you. So Emma was taken away as well – a lady friend for Morgane. The four-way ménage works very well. The master and mistress
work together on photographic projects. And the dogs are always with
them. Master is the photographer and the mistress handles the styling, the business side of the venture, and their press and public relations. And can she ever cook! Mostly in Berlin, because the flat is big
enough to take a lot of guests. What she'd love most, though, would
be to cook in France, on a farm of her own. It's a dream the dogs and
their owners share, and that is why the style of their interior recalls
that of a French country house.

Morgane & Emma

Morgane und Emma haben mehrere Zuhause. Eine kleine Wohnung in Paris, die schönste in Berlin und dann noch eine in Miami.
Das ist eigentlich ihre Heimat, falls man ein Tierheim so nennen
kann. Aber Gott sei Dank hat das Herrchen sie herausgeholt. Erst
Morgane. Später kam er wieder. Mit seiner Freundin. Weil er wohl
gemerkt hatte, dass zu zweit alles viel lustiger ist, wurde Emma
aus dem Tierheim geholt – als Freundin für Morgane. Die Vierer-
beziehung klappt gut. Herrchen und Frauchen arbeiten zusammen,
für Fotoproduktionen. Und die Hunde sind immer dabei. Er ist
Fotograf, sie macht Styling, außerdem das Geschäftliche, Presse-
und Öffentlichkeitsarbeit. Und kochen kann sie! Meistens in Berlin,
weil die Wohnung groß genug ist für viele Gäste. Aber am liebsten
würde sie in Frankreich kochen, auf einem eigenen Bauernhof. Das
wäre der Traum der Hunde und ihrer Besitzer und deshalb erinnert
ihre Einrichtung auch an den französischen Landhausstil.

Morgane et Emma ont un bel appartement à Berlin, un pied-à-terre
à Paris et un autre logement à Miami, ce dernier étant à proprement
parler leur patrie, si on peut appeler ainsi un refuge pour animaux.
Mais Dieu merci, elles en sont sorties. D'abord le maître est venu
chercher Morgane. Ensuite, il est revenu avec son amie – sans doute
avait-il remarqué que tout est beaucoup plus gai à deux –, et ils ont
emmené Emma. Ils s'entendent bien tous les quatre. Les maîtres tra-
vaillent ensemble pour des productions photographiques – et les chiens
sont toujours à leurs côtés. Il est photographe, elle veille au styling et
aux affaires, aux relations publiques. Et puis elle est un vrai cordon-
bleu, surtout à Berlin, car l'appartement est vaste et peut accueillir
de nombreux invités. Mais c'est en France qu'elle aimerait faire la
cuisine, dans sa ferme à elle. Ce serait le rêve des chiens et de leurs
propriétaires, et c'est pour cela que leur intérieur évoque une maison
de campagne française.

When they aren't having tea, playing cards, watching television or engaging in long discussions, the members of the "Gürün Solidarity Association" like to spend their free time at the sports club, "KSF Umut Spor" – literally, Kreuzberg Sport Fans. The café is their clubhouse, as it were, and they run it on an unpaid basis. And they are going on trips together if the Turkish national soccer side has a match somewhere in Germany. Or at times they counsel fellow countrymen with problems. All are welcome at the café, including women. But women rarely come, despite the fact that "KSF Umut Spor" even has a ladies' soccer team. Most of the young women who play soccer here can hardly imagine nowadays, that for their fathers' generation, meeting places such as the Association's café once represented a piece of home from home. And, for that generation, still does.

Türkisches Vereinscafé

Wenn sie nicht Tee trinken, Karten spielen, Fernsehen schauen oder diskutieren, dann verbringen die Mitglieder vom »Solidaritätsverein aus Gürün« ihre Freizeit gern im Sportverein »KSF Umut Spor«. Das Café ist sozusagen ihr Clubhaus, das sie in ehrenamtlicher Arbeit betreiben. Und sie reisen gemeinsam, wenn die türkische Nationalmannschaft irgendwo in Deutschland spielt. Oder beraten auch manchmal Landsleute bei Problemen. Willkommen ist jeder im Café, auch Frauen. Aber Frauen kommen selten, obwohl der »KSF Umut Spor« sogar eine Damenfußballmannschaft hat. Von den jungen Spielerinnen können sich die meisten gar nicht mehr vorstellen, dass für ihre Väter Treffpunkte wie das Vereinscafé ein Stück importierter Heimat war. Und noch ist.

Quand ils ne sont pas en train de boire du thé, de jouer aux cartes, de regarder la télévision ou de discuter, les membres de «l'Amicale de Gurun» se retrouvent volontiers au «KSF Umut Spor», l'association des «Amis des sports de Kreuzberg». Le café est pour ainsi dire leur club. Des volontaires servent du thé, font le ménage, organisent des barbecues et partent en voyage ensemble quand l'équipe nationale turque joue quelque part en Allemagne. Ou bien, quelquefois, ils donnent des conseils à des compatriotes en difficultés. Tout le monde est bienvenu ici, les femmes aussi. Mais elles font rarement leur apparition bien que «KSF Umut Spor» ait aussi une équipe de football féminine. La plupart des jeunes joueuses ne peuvent pas s'imaginer que pour leurs pères, rencontrer des compatriotes dans des endroits comme ce café c'était un peu se retrouver au pays – et qu'il en est toujours ainsi.

Sabina Nordalm finds Berlin ideal for her work. "Everything is possible here, the city is really vibrant and open for new things." New things such as furniture sculpture, which Nordalm designs for her company "raumwerk" and has built before putting the finishing touches to the pieces in her own kitchen. At a joiner's bench that has taken six people to carry up, boards are polished and simple pinewood is impregnated with pigmented oil till it acquires a finer sheen than that of costly woods. Behind the pink doors of the kitchen, which she designed herself, there's not just crockery but also tools and a chainsaw. This last is a relic of her sculptural studies, since Sabina Nordalm has more need of her mind than of dangerous implements when she makes furniture. What she enjoys is deliberating upon combinations of different materials and colours or individually suiting her furniture to the rooms it is intended for. Her apartment is her experimental lab – for the creation of the perfect design.

Sabina Nordalm

Sabina Nordalm findet Berlin für ihre Arbeit ideal. »Weil hier alles möglich ist, weil die Stadt förmlich vibriert und offen ist für Neues.« Zum Beispiel für Möbelskulpturen, die Nordalm für ihre Firma »raumwerk« entwirft, die sie vorfertigen lässt und denen sie in ihrer Küche den letzten Schliff gibt. An einer Hobelbank, die sechs Leute hochgeschleppt haben, werden Baubohlen poliert und einfaches Tannenholz mit pigmentversetztem Öl geweißt, bis es edler schimmert als teure Hölzer. Hinter den rosa Türen ihrer selbst entworfenen Küche stapeln sich nicht nur Geschirr, sondern Werkzeug und eine Kettensäge. Ein Relikt aus ihrem Bildhauerstudium, denn für ihre Möbelobjekte braucht Sabina Nordalm eher ihren Kopf als martialische Gerätschaften. Weil sie über die Kombination verschiedener Materialien und Farben nachgrübelt oder weil sie ihre Möbel individuell auf Räume abstimmen will. Ihre Wohnung ist dafür Versuchslabor – für die Entwicklung des perfekten Designs.

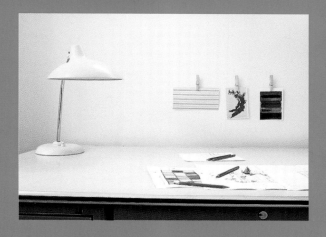

Sabina Nordalm trouve Berlin idéale pour travailler. «Parce qu'ici tout est possible; la ville vibre littéralement et est ouverte à la nouveauté.» Par exemple aux meubles-sculptures qu'elle crée pour sa firme «raumwerk», et qu'elle fait préfabriquer avant de les fignoler dans sa cuisine. Sur un établi que six personnes ont monté chez elle, elle polit des madriers et blanchit du bois de sapin avec une huile mélangée de pigments jusqu'à ce qu'il ait l'air d'une essence précieuse. Les portes roses de la cuisine fabriquée par ses soins ne dissimulent pas seulement la vaisselle mais aussi des outils et une scie à chaîne. Un souvenir de ses études de sculpteur, car pour créer ses meubles-objets, c'est de sa tête que Sabina a le plus besoin. Parce qu'elle médite au mariage de différents matériaux et couleurs ou parce qu'elle veut harmoniser de manière individuelle ses meubles aux pièces. Son appartement est son laboratoire – c'est ici qu'elle tente de mettre au point le design parfait.

Hans Rosenthal's children's show "Kleine Leute – grosse Klasse"
(Little Folks, Big Style) and his quiz show "Allein gegen alle" (One
Against All) earned him a popular vote as Germany's favourite television presenter. "He is the sort of fellow you could chat to across the
garden fence," the eulogy on that occasion declared. For Rosenthal
the words must have had an ironic sound to them. The fact was that
he had actually lived in a garden for two years. But at a time when
no one chatted to him. Rosenthal was Jewish, and survived the Nazi
years in a humble summerhouse in the "Am Volkspark Prenzlauer
Berg e.V." allotment gardens, where two old ladies had hidden him.
That summerhouse has survived, and the 384 members of the gardens association are proud to this day of that unseen neighbour who
only emerged from his place of concealment when the air raid sirens
sounded. Other allotment gardeners have also had their lives saved
by their little plots of land. In times of scarcity, they lived in huts they
had built themselves, eating vegetables they grew in their own gardens.

Schrebergärten

Seine Kindersendung hieß »Kleine Leute – große Klasse«, seine
Quizshow war »Allein gegen alle«. Dafür wurde Hans Rosenthal
zum beliebtesten Fernsehmoderator Deutschlands gewählt. »Er
ist der typische Gartennachbar. Mit dem kann man reden …«, hieß
es in der Laudatio. Muss für Rosenthal komisch geklungen haben.
Denn er war wirklich zwei Jahre lang Gartenbewohner. Aber reden
konnte man nicht mit ihm. Der Jude Rosenthal überlebte nämlich
die Nazizeit in einer Laube der Gartenkolonie »Am Volkspark Prenzlauer Berg e.V.«, versteckt von zwei alten Damen. Die Laube steht
noch und die 384 Gartenvereinsmitglieder sind heute stolz auf
ihren unsichtbaren Nachbarn, der sein Versteck nur bei Bomben-
alarm verließ. Auch anderen Kleingärtnern hat ihr Stück Land das
Leben gerettet. Weil sie in Notzeiten dort lebten und sich vom an-
gebauten Gemüse ernährten. Auch heute wird in den ehemaligen
»Armengärten« noch Gemüse angebaut. Als Freizeitspaß.

Son émission enfantine «Kleine Leute – grosse Klasse» (Petits
hommes – grande classe) et son quiz «Allein gegen alle» (Un contre
tous) firent de Hans Rosenthal l'animateur favori des téléspectateurs.
Il n'empêche que l'éloge qu'on lui a adressé, «Il est le voisin de jardin
typique. On peut parler avec lui …», a dû sonner bizarrement à ses
oreilles, parce que s'il s'est vraiment mis au vert pendant deux ans,
il essayait alors plutôt d'éviter les bavardages. En effet, Rosenthal est
juif et n'a pu échapper aux nazis que parce que deux vieilles dames
l'ont dissimulé dans une cabane des jardins ouvriers «Am Volkspark
Prenzlauer Berg e.V.». La cabane est toujours là et les 384 membres
de l'association sont aujourd'hui fiers de leur voisin invisible. Leur petit bout de terrain a aussi sauvé la vie à d'autres petits jardiniers qui
vivaient dans leurs cabanes quand les temps étaient difficiles et se
nourrissaient de ce qu'ils récoltaient. Aujourd'hui on cultive encore
des légumes dans les anciens «jardins des pauvres». Pour se distraire.

Eingangsseiten: *Während der Nazizeit hielt sich Hans Rosenthal zwei Jahre lang in dieser Laube versteckt.*
Vorhergehende Doppelseite: *Details in der ältesten Laube der Schrebergartensiedlung »Am Volkspark Prenzlauer Berg«.*
Oben: *Viele alte Möbel sind noch erhalten, »neu« ist allerdings die Stehlampe aus den 1950er Jahren.*
Rechts: *1903 zog die Großmutter des jetzigen Laubenbesitzers in ihr 30 Quadratmeter großes Haus ein.*
Rechte Seite: *Das Sofa diente nachts als Bett.*

First pages: *During the Nazi Reich, Hans Rosenthal was concealed in this summerhouse for two years.*
Previous pages: *details of the oldest summerhouse on this colony of allotment gardens.*
Above: *Many old items of furniture have survived, though the standard lamp is "new", dating from the 1950s.*
Right: *In 1903 the grandmother of the current owner of the summerhouse took possession of her 30 square metres.*
Facing page: *At night the sofa served as a bed.*

Premières pages: *Hans Rosenthal est resté caché deux ans dans cette cabane de jardin.*
Double page précédente: *détails de la plus ancienne cabane des jardins ouvriers «Am Volkspark Prenzlauer Berg».*
Ci-dessus: *Le lampadaire date des années 1950.*
A droite: *En 1903, la grand-mère de l'actuel propriétaire s'installa dans ces 30 mètres carrés.*
Page de droite: *Le canapé servait aussi de lit.*

Charlottenburg

Franz Kafka wrote, Robert Stolz composed and Helmut Newton took photographs at the Askanischer Hof. Günter Pfitzmann even acted in the hotel for the duration of an entire series. But of course it is possible simply to stay at the Askanischer Hof, as the likes of Michel Piccoli, David Bowie, Walter de Maria, Bob Wilson or Anthony Quinn have done – or anyone requiring a room. "We have a lot of regular architects and theatre and film people who always book the same room," says Eva Glinicke, who bought the hotel in 1963. She takes particular pride in the furniture. Just recently she found a complete Swedish Art Nouveau bedroom suite dating from 1905. At an auction she purchased for the breakfast room the chairs and armchairs once in the possession of Schlosshotel Gerhus – "which Kaiser Wilhelm sat on". The 16 rooms of the Art Nouveau building, with its crooked passageways, have state of the art fittings, however, from ISDN phone lines to well-lit make-up mirrors.

Askanischer Hof

Franz Kafka schrieb, Robert Stolz komponierte und Helmut Newton fotografierte im Askanischen Hof. Und Günter Pfitzmann schauspielerte im Hotel sogar eine ganze Serie lang. Man kann dort aber auch einfach nur wohnen und schlafen, wie beispielsweise Michel Piccoli, David Bowie, Walter de Maria, Bob Wilson oder Anthony Quinn. Oder wie jeder, der ein Zimmer bestellt. »Zu uns kommen viele Architekten, Theater- und Filmleute, die immer dieselben Zimmer buchen«, erzählt Eva Glinicke, die das Hotel 1963 kaufte. Besonders stolz ist sie auf die Einrichtung. Erst neulich hat sie ein schwedisches Jugendstilschlafzimmer von 1905 gefunden. Oder sie ersteigerte für den Frühstücksraum die Sessel und Stühle des ehemaligen Schlosshotels Gerhus, »auf denen der Kaiser schon gesessen hat«. Die 16 Zimmer im Jugendstilhaus mit den verwinkelten Fluren sind allerdings technisch top ausgerüstet: mit ISDN-Anschlüssen und gut beleuchteten Schminkspiegeln.

Franz Kafka a écrit, Robert Stolz composé et Helmut Newton photographié à l'Askanischer Hof. Et Günter Pfitzmann y a tourné toute une série télévisée. Mais on peut aussi simplement habiter et dormir dans cet hôtel comme l'ont fait ou le font par exemple Anthony Quinn, Michel Piccoli, David Bowie, Walter de Maria et Bob Wilson ou tous ceux qui réservent une chambre. «Beaucoup d'architectes, de gens du théâtre et du cinéma viennent chez nous et veulent toujours la même chambre», raconte Eva Glinicke qui a acheté l'hôtel en 1963. Elle est particulièrement fière de l'ameublement. Dernièrement elle a trouvé une chambre à coucher Jugendstil suédoise de 1905. Et puis elle acheté aux enchères pour le salon du petit déjeuner les fauteuils et les chaises de l'ancien Schlosshotel Gerhus, – le Kaiser s'y est déjà assis. Il n'empêche que les 16 chambres de la maison Jugendstil aux corridors tortueux sont très bien équipées, avec des prises RNIS et des miroirs à maquillage bien éclairés.

Fahrräder
abstellen verboten

Eingangsseite: *prächtiger Eingang zum Jugendstilhotel, in dem die Zeit stehen geblieben zu sein scheint.*
Vorhergehende Doppelseite: *Früher standen die Sessel und Stühle des Frühstücksraums im Schlosshotel Gerhus.*
Linke Seite: *Zimmer Nr. 15 ist riesengroß.*
Oben und rechts: *Einzelzimmer Nr. 24 mit Möbeln und breitem Bett im Chippendale-Stil. Die blau-rot-weiß bekränzte Lampe beleuchtet den kleinen Erker, die sachliche gibt Licht am Tisch.*

First page: *the majestic entrance to this Art Nouveau hotel, where time truly seems to have stood still.*
Previous pages: *The chairs and armchairs in the breakfast room were formerly in the Schlosshotel Gerhus.*
Facing page: *Room number 15 is of a substantial size.*
Above and right: *single room number 24, with furniture and king-size bed in Chippendale style. The lamp garlanded in red, white and blue lights the niche, the other sheds light at the table.*

Première page: *la superbe entrée de l'hôtel Jugendstil, où le temps semble s'être arrêté.*
Double page précédente: *Les fauteuils et les chaises du salon du petit déjeuner viennent du Schlosshotel Gerhus.*
Page de gauche: *La chambre n° 15 est immense.*
Ci-dessus et à droite: *la chambre simple n° 24 – les meubles et le large lit de style Chippendale. La lampe entourée d'une guirlande bleu-rouge-blanc éclaire le petit bow-window, le sobre lampadaire illumine la table.*

First he simply gave a girlfriend's apartment a more stylish look. Then he helped the girlfriend's girlfriend pick her furniture. Then the girlfriend's girlfriend's girlfriend. And that, says Stefan Fuhrmann, is how he came to interior design. "All of a sudden," he says, "I was selling ideas for the home." He likes to start by talking to clients in need of counsel, preferably over coffee and cake, and then by flipping through books and home magazines with them. Once a fundamental agreement has been achieved, Fuhrmann organizes the changes. For one schooled in interior decorating and a self-confessed perfectionist who prefers to establish a thematic motif for an entire apartment, it's not an easy business. But no effort is too great: for one client he papered his own bright red apartment with black and white stripes, because she was simply unable to envisage what stripes would look like. "It was no use," recalls Fuhrmann cheerfully, "to this day I've never managed to sell anyone on stripes."

Stefan Fuhrmann

Erst hatte er nur die Wohnung einer Freundin aufgepeppt, dann half er der Freundin der Freundin bei der Inneneinrichtung und dann deren Freundin. So erzählt Stefan Fuhrmann seinen Einstieg ins Interior Design. »Plötzlich«, sagt er, »war ich einer, der Wohnideen verkauft.« Einer, der mit Ratsuchenden erst mal redet, am liebsten bei Kaffee und Kuchen, dann mit ihnen Bücher und Wohnzeitschriften wälzt. Wenn ein Grundkonsens da ist, organisiert Fuhrmann die Umgestaltung. Kein leichtes Geschäft für den gelernten Dekorateur, der sich als Perfektionist bezeichnet und am liebsten immer »einen roten Faden«, ein Thema, in der Wohnung inszenieren möchte. Dafür ist ihm kein Aufwand zu groß: Für eine Kundin beklebte er seine eigene knallrote Wohnung überall mit schwarzweißen Streifen – weil sie sich partout keine Streifen vorstellen konnte. »Nützte nichts«, sagt Fuhrmann fröhlich, »bis heute habe ich keinem Menschen Streifen verkaufen können.«

Au départ, il avait arrangé l'appartement d'une amie, après il a aidé l'amie de cette amie à décorer le sien et puis son amie à elle. C'est ainsi, raconte Stefan Fuhrman qu'il est entré dans la profession. «Soudain, j'étais quelqu'un qui vendait des idées de décoration intérieure.» Quelqu'un qui commence par s'entretenir avec ceux qui viennent lui demander conseil, de préférence devant une tasse de café et une tranche de gâteau, avant de consulter avec eux des tas de livres et de magazines de décoration. Quand ils s'entendent sur le fond des choses, Fuhrmann se met au travail. Il se considère comme un perfectionniste et aimerait suivre toujours «un fil rouge», un thème qu'il pourrait mettre en scène dans l'appartement. Pour cela, rien ne le rebute: une de ses clientes étant incapable de s'imaginer leur effet, il a collé partout des bandes noires dans son propre appartement rouge vif. «Pour rien», dit Fuhrmann joyeusement, «jusqu'ici je n'ai encore vendu de bandes à personne.»

Eingangsseite: verspiegeltes Kunststoffrelief.
Vorhergehende Doppelseite: zwei hängende »Bubble«-Sessel aus Kunststoff und ein ausgestopfter Tierkopf namens »Eddie«.
Oben: alte Leuchtreklame-Buchstaben aus einem Milchladen.
Rechts: zwei schwarze »Wassily«-Sessel im Schlafzimmer.
Rechte Seite: Im Gästezimmer steht ein Bett aus den 1920er Jahren.
Folgende Doppelseite: Im Bad malte Fuhrmann die Streifen noch auf die Wand, für sein Schlafzimmer fand er gestreifte Tapete.

First page: reflecting synthetic relief.
Previous pages: two suspended synthetic "Bubble" chairs and a stuffed animal's head (known as "Eddie").
Above: The letters spelling "milk" are from the old neon logo at a dairy store.
Right: two black "Wassily" chairs in the bedroom.
Facing page: In the guest room is a bed dating from the 1920s.
Following pages: Whereas the stripes in the bedroom were wallpaper, here in the bathroom Fuhrmann painted them onto the wall.

Première page: relief en matière synthétique miroitante.
Double page précédente: deux chaises «Bubble» suspendues en matière plastique et «Eddie» – une tête d'animal empaillée.
Ci-dessus: les lettres en plastique d'une ancienne enseigne lumineuse.
A droite: deux chaises «Wassily» noires dans la chambre à coucher.
Page de droite: dans la chambre d'hôte, un lit des années 1920.
Double page suivante: Les rayures de la salle de bains sont peintes à même le mur; pour la chambre à coucher Fuhrmann a trouvé du papier peint rayé.

Berlin Interiors   Stefan Fuhrmann

In late 1993, Cologne art dealer Max Hetzler and his wife, art dealer Samia Saouma, moved from Paris to Berlin. "It was obvious that Berlin was going to be the most interesting city for young artists – a big city, with history, low rents, and an urban feel," says Hetzler. The couple rented a huge factory loft in the west end of the city, where they lived and exhibited the work of their artists. When Max junior was born, Saouma and Hetzler separated their working and private lives, albeit only in terms of physical space. Naturally they live with their art, and equally naturally the steady flow of visitors to Berlin are invited to the Hetzlers'. "Feedback from the outside world is of enormous importance for the gallery and for one's own thinking," says Hetzler: "it's how we know we're in the right place."

Max Hetzler &
Samia Saouma

Ende 1993 zogen der Galerist Max Hetzler von Köln und seine Frau, die Galeristin Samia Saouma, von Paris nach Berlin. »Es war klar, dass Berlin für junge Künstler die interessanteste Stadt sein würde – Großstadt, Geschichte, billige Mieten, urbanes Umfeld«, sagt Hetzler. Die beiden mieteten sich im Westen der Stadt einen riesigen Fabrikloft, lebten dort und stellten die Arbeiten ihrer Künstler aus. Nachdem Max junior geboren wurde, trennten Saouma und Hetzler Arbeit und Wohnen, allerdings nur räumlich. Denn natürlich leben sie mit ihrer Kunst, und selbstverständlich werden die vielen Besucher zu Hetzlers geladen. »Resonanz von außen ist enorm wichtig für die Galerie und für den Kopf«, sagt Hetzler, »daran merkt man, dass wir am richtigen Ort sind.«

Le galeriste Max Hetzler, de Cologne, et son épouse, la galeriste Samia Saouma, de Paris, sont arrivés à Berlin fin 1993. «On savait que Berlin serait la ville la plus intéressante pour les jeunes créateurs – métropole, histoire, loyers bon marché, environnement urbain», dit Hetzler. Ils louèrent à l'ouest de la ville un immense loft d'usine, pour y vivre et y exposer les travaux des artistes. Depuis la naissance de Max junior, Saouma et Hetzler ont séparé travail et vie privée, mais uniquement sur le plan spatial. Car ils vivent avec leur art. «La résonance extérieure a une importance énorme», dit Hetzler, «elle nous montre que nous sommes au bon endroit.»

Vorhergehende Doppelseite: *Die klassische Altbauwohnung ist mit modernen Möbelklassikern eingerichtet: rotbeige Bett-Couch von Jean Prouvé, zwei Sessel von Harry Bertoia, Sofa von Florence Knoll. Links ein Gemälde von Albert Oehlen, geradeaus ein Bild von Christopher Wool.*
Rechts: *Blick vom Wohnzimmer in die Bibliothek.*
Unten: *Samia Saouma und Max Hetzler haben ihre Bücher und Kunstkataloge in einfachen Stahlregalen untergebracht. Zwischen den Fenstern hängt ein Gemälde von Martin Kippenberger, auf dem Tisch steht die »Puppy«-Vase von Jeff Koons.*

Previous pages: *The classic apartment in an old building is furnished with modern classics: a ginger-beige bed-settee by Jean Prouvé, two deep chairs by Harry Bertoia and a sofa by Florence Knoll. The painting on the left is by Albert Oehlen, the one straight ahead is by Christopher Wool.*
Right: *looking from the living room into the library.*
Below: *Samia Saouma and Max Hetzler's books and art catalogues are on simple steel shelving. Between the windows is a painting by Martin Kippenberger and on the table is the "puppy" vase by Jeff Koons.*

Double page précédente: *L'appartement abrite des classiques modernes: un lit de repos rouge/beige de Jean Prouvé, deux fauteuils de Harry Bertoia, un canapé de Florence Knoll. A gauche, une toile d'Albert Oehlen, au fond un tableau de Christopher Wool.*
A droite: *la bibliothèque vue du séjour.*
Ci-dessous: *Les livres et les catalogues d'art sont rangés dans des étagères d'acier toutes simples. Entre les fenêtres, un tableau de Martin Kippenberger, sur la table le vase «Puppy» de Jeff Koons.*

Oben: *Esszimmer mit einem Glasschrank von Mathis Esterhazy aus den 1980er Jahren. Um den Tisch stehen sechs Stühle des Wiener Künstlers Franz West. Auf dem Sockel eine Skulptur von Paul McCarthy.*
Rechts: *dreibeiniger Tisch von Jean Prouvé, das Bild im Esszimmer ist von Günther Förg.*

Above: *the dining room, with a 1980s glass cabinet by Mathis Esterhazy. The six dining chairs are by Viennese artist Franz West. The sculpture on the plinth is by Paul McCarthy.*
Right: *The three-legged table is by Jean Prouvé. The picture in the dining room is by Günther Förg.*

Ci-dessus *La salle à manger abrite une armoire vitrée de Mathis Esterhazy des années 1980. Autour de la table, six chaises de l'artiste viennois Franz West. Sur le socle, une sculpture de Paul McCarthy.*
A droite: *une table trépied de Jean Prouvé; le tableau de la salle à manger est signé Günther Förg.*

Linke Seite: Der Teppich von Albert Oehlen ist ein Einzelstück.
Oben: Kinderzimmer von Max junior.
Rechts: Stahl-Lagerregale mit Büchern auch im Flur.
Folgende Doppelseite: Tisch, Stuhl und Schrank im Schlafzimmer
sind von Jean Prouvé. Über dem Schreibtisch von Charles Eames ein
Bild des Berliners Michel Majerus.

Facing page: The carpet by Albert Oehlen is a unique piece.
Above: Max junior's room.
Right: In the passage there are more steel bookshelves.
Following pages: The table, chair and cupboard in the bedroom are
by Jean Prouvé. Over the Charles Eames desk is a picture by Berlin
artist Michel Majerus.

Page de gauche: Le tapis d'Albert Oehlen est une pièce unique.
Ci-dessus: la chambre de Max junior.
A droite: dans le couloir aussi, des étagères en acier pour les livres.
Double page suivante: La table, la chaise et l'armoire de la chambre
à coucher sont de Jean Prouvé. Au-dessus du bureau de Charles Eames
un tableau du Berlinois Michel Majerus.

Hans-Peter Jochum didn't care for the room-plan of his new flat in Charlottenburg at all. He bought it nonetheless, because he liked the quiet location. Even walking there, he says, he can switch off – "away from the street, across the courtyard, up to the side wing of the fourth floor, then three more steps up to the flat". Conversion was elaborate and bade farewell to most of the walls, but now Jochum feels he has a secluded retreat that suits his requirements perfectly. "I don't spend much time in the flat, so I don't need many things around me," he says; and the fact is that in his two galleries for 20th century design he is constantly surrounded by beautiful items of furniture. He planned the conversion with architect Thomas Kröger – a generous room-plan with light, grey linoleum floors and papyrus-white walls, with no ceiling lights and only a single light switch in the hall.

Hans-Peter Jochum

Den Grundriss seiner neuen Wohnung in Charlottenburg mochte Hans-Peter Jochum überhaupt nicht. Trotzdem kaufte er sie, weil ihm die ruhige Lage gefiel. Schon auf dem Weg dorthin, sagt Jochum, könne er abschalten, »weg von der Straße, über den Hof in die vierte Etage im Seitenflügel und dann noch drei Stufen in die Wohnung«. Nach dem Umbau, in dem fast alle Wände fielen, fühlt sich Jochum wie in einer Klause, die genau auf seine Bedürfnisse zugeschnitten ist. »Ich brauche in der knappen Zeit, die ich in meiner Wohnung verbringe, nicht so viele Dinge um mich herum«, sagt er, denn er hat täglich in seinen zwei Galerien für Designobjekte des 20. Jahrhunderts mit schönen Möbeln zu tun. Zusammen mit dem Architekten Thomas Kröger plante er den Wohnungsumbau – einen großzügigen Grundriss mit hellem, grauen Linoleum-Fußboden und papyrusweißen Wänden, ohne Deckenleuchten und mit nur einem einzigen Lichtschalter im Eingangsbereich.

Hans-Peter Jochum n'aimait pas du tout le plan de son nouvel appartement de Charlottenburg, mais il l'avait acheté parce que l'endroit où il se trouvait était calme. Le chemin pour s'y rendre était déjà apaisant, «laisser la rue derrière soi, traverser la cour, monter au quatrième étage dans l'aile latérale, ensuite trois marches et on entre dans l'appartement». Après des travaux approfondis au cours desquels presque tous les murs ont été abattus, Jochum a l'impression de vivre dans une cellule qui répond parfaitement à ses besoins. «Vu le peu de temps que je passe dans mon appartement, je n'ai pas besoin de beaucoup de choses autour de moi», dit-il car il côtoie tous les jours de beaux meubles dans ses deux galeries consacrées au design du 20e siècle. Avec la complicité de l'architecte Thomas Kröger, il a mis au point les transformations – des espaces généreux avec un sol de linoléum gris clair et des murs blancs papyrus, sans plafonniers et avec un seul interrupteur dans l'entrée.

Vorhergehende Doppelseite: *Der Eingangsbereich öffnet sich zur Küche. Natürlich lebt Jochum mit modernen Klassikern: Die orangen Stühle von Charles Eames sind von 1952, den Tisch hat Florence Knoll 1955 entworfen und die Stehlampen gestaltete Gino Sarfatti 1956.*
Oben: *Blick vom Eingang durch die gesamte Wohnung. Rechts der offene Küchenraum, dahinter das eingestellte Bad und im Hintergrund ein wandfüllender Schrank mit Schiebetüren, in dem alle Gebrauchsgegenstände verschwinden.*
Rechts: *Tisch des Dänen Hans Wegner von 1951 aus massiver Eiche. Die beiden Stühle von Eames sind mit Wollstoff bezogen.*

Previous pages: *The hall opens directly onto the kitchen. Naturally, Jochum is surrounded by modern classics: the two orange chairs by Charles Eames date from 1952, the Florence Knoll table from 1955, and the Gino Sarfatti standard lamps from 1956.*
Above: *looking from the hall into the flat, the open kitchen is to the right and beyond it the bathroom. Ahead is a wall-length cupboard with sliding doors to accommodate everyday utility objects.*
Right: *The 1951 oak table is by Denmark's Hans Wegner. The two chairs by Eames have woollen coverings.*

Double page précédente: *L'entrée s'ouvre sur la cuisine. Jochum vit bien sûr au milieu de grands classiques modernes: les deux chaises orange de Charles Eames sont de 1952, la table a été dessinée par Florence Knoll en 1955 et les lampadaires sont signés Gino Sarfatti (1956).*
Ci-dessus: *tout l'appartement vu de l'entrée. A droite la cuisine ouverte, derrière la salle de bains et à l'arrière-plan un placard mural à portes coulissantes dans lequel disparaissent tous les objets utilitaires.*
A droite: *une table de 1951 en chêne massif du Danois Hans Wegner. Les deux chaises d'Eames sont recouvertes de lainage.*

Berlin Interiors   Hans-Peter Jochum

Rechts: Das Sofa von Mario Bellini, 1966 für Cassina entworfen, hat einen neuen Bezug bekommen. Die Lampe entwarf Arne Jacobsen 1958 für ein Hotel. An der Wand zwei Bilder von Thomas Grünfeld.
Unten: *Tragende Stützen statt der früheren Wand machen die Wohnung großzügig. Die Edelstahl-Lichtskulptur an der Wand hat Gianfranco Fini 1968 gebaut.*
Folgende Doppelseite: *Im Bad wurden die Wände nicht gefliest, sondern mit papyrusweißem Lack gestrichen, der Fußboden ist ein gegossener Kunstharz-Estrich.*

Right: *The Mario Bellini sofa, designed for Cassina in 1966, has been re-covered. The lamp was intended for a hotel when Arne Jacobsen designed it in 1958. On the wall are two pictures by Thomas Grünfeld.*
Below: *Weight-bearing columns have replaced the walls that previously existed and make the apartment more spacious. The stainless steel light sculpture on the wall was made by Gianfranco Fini in 1968.*
Following pages: *The bathroom walls were not tiled but instead varnished with papyrus-white lacquer. The floor is surfaced with synthetic resin.*

A droite: *Le canapé de Mario Bellini, dessiné en 1966 pour Cassina, a été habillé de neuf. La lampe a été prévue par Arne Jacobsen en 1958 pour un hôtel. Sur le mur, deux tableaux de Thomas Grünfeld.*
Ci-dessous: *Les colonnes qui remplacent le mur abattu rendent l'appartement plus vaste. La sculpture lumineuse en acier spécial sur le mur a été réalisée en 1968 par Gianfranco Fini.*
Double page suivante: *Les murs de la salle de bains ne sont pas carrelés mais peints en blanc papyrus, le sol est recouvert d'un enduit synthétique.*

Two years before the Wall fell, Rudolf Harbord found his apartment. Five rooms, a large balcony, not far from the Technical University, where he teaches. Harbord bought the flat and was already planning the renovation when the nightmare began: there were problems with the purchase contract, the seller was untraceable, the money was gone, a law suit followed, and the law's delays. Ingeborg Wiensowski, Harbord's partner, hit on the idea of mounting exhibitions in the empty rooms. The first art show at Harbord & Wiensowski was in 1989. Since then there have been more than 50 exhibitions. And they have come to delight at living in empty rooms full of art. "All you need is a chair, a table and a bed," says Harbord. Not that it's quite as spartan as that sounds – each of them has another (furnished) home.

Rudolf Harbord & Ingeborg Wiensowski

Zwei Jahre vor der Wende fand Rudolf Harbord seine Wohnung. Fünf Zimmer, großer Balkon, nicht weit zur Technischen Universität, wo er lehrt. Harbord kaufte und plante schon die Renovierung. Dann begann der Alptraum: Probleme mit dem Kaufvertrag, Verkäufer unauffindbar, Geld weg, Klage, langsame Gerichte. Ingeborg Wiensowski, Harbords Lebensgefährtin, kam auf die Idee, in den leeren Räumen Ausstellungen zu zeigen. Die erste Kunstschau bei Harbord & Wiensowski fand 1989 statt. Seitdem gab es über 50 Ausstellungen. Inzwischen finden sie es wunderbar, in leeren Räumen mit der Kunst zu leben. »Man braucht nur Stuhl, Tisch und Bett«, sagt Harbord. Ganz so asketisch, wie es klingt, ist es nicht, denn beide haben noch einen anderen Wohnsitz – einen möblierten.

Rudolf Harbord a déniché son appartement deux ans avant la chute du mur de Berlin. Cinq pièces, un grand balcon, à deux pas de l'I.U.T. où il enseigne. Il l'a acheté et commençait à faire des projets de rénovation. Et puis le cauchemar a commencé: difficultés avec le contrat, vendeur introuvable, argent disparu, plainte, lenteur des tribunaux. Sa compagne, Ingeborg Wiensowski, a eu alors l'idée de monter des expositions dans les pièces vides. La première eut lieu en 1989. Depuis, plus de 50 expositions se sont déroulées ici. Ils trouvent merveilleux de vivre avec l'art dans des pièces vides. «On n'a besoin que d'une chaise, d'une table et d'un lit», dit Harbord. Ne prenons pas cet ascétisme à la lettre, car ils disposent d'un autre logement, meublé celui-là.

Eingangsseite: drei leere ineinander übergehende Zimmer. Im Hintergrund eine Fotoarbeit von Alexander Vethers.
Vorhergehende Doppelseite: Im »Berliner Zimmer« wird manchmal das Fernsehgerät aufgestellt. Die Fotos sind von Alexander Vethers.
Oben: Im Schlafzimmer hängen Arbeiten aus früheren Ausstellungen, beispielsweise »Edelweiß« von Sabina Streeter.
Rechts: Kleiderstange und gefundener Gartentisch als Ablage im Flur.
Rechte Seite: Gemälde von Matthias Schaufler.

First page: a suite of three empty rooms, with a photographic work by Alexander Vethers visible at the end.
Previous pages: The television is sometimes installed in the "Berlin Room". The photos are by Alexander Vethers.
Above: In the bedroom are works from earlier exhibitions, such as Sabina Streeter's "Edelweiß".
Right: in the hall is a simple coat-rail, with a found garden table for occasional purposes.
Facing page: The painting is by Matthias Schaufler.

Première page: trois pièces vides en enfilade. Au fond, une photographie d'Alexander Vethers.
Double page précédente: Dans la «pièce berlinoise», on installe quelquefois la télévision. Les photographies sont d'Alexander Vethers.
Ci-dessus: La chambre à coucher accueille des travaux d'anciennes expositions, par exemple «Edelweiß» de Sabina Streeter.
A droite: Dans le couloir une tringle à vêtements côtoie une table de jardin.
Page de droite: tableau de Matthias Schaufler.

Berlin Interiors   Rudolf Harbord & Ingeborg Wiensowski

If there were an award for people who make the impossible possible in the remotest parts of the world, Gisela von Schenk would have won it. For instance, in the tropical jungles of Peru she fitted out a house with furniture that did not exist in that region, with articles that others considered junk, and with fabrics that no one in that country had ever set eyes on. Her husband would tremble whenever she set off yet again to the back of beyond in quest of unusual furniture. When the task was finally completed, the von Schenks were expropriated by the military regime. First they moved to New York, subsequently returning to Europe. For two years, Gisela von Schenk has once again been living in the city of her birth, Berlin. Together with Frank Stüve she exhibits concepts in interior design at her stylish Grunewald villa. "The lightness of being" is the motto she has chosen for her own furnishings: "At home I feel as if I'm in a nest."

Gisela von Schenk

Wenn es einen Orden gäbe für Leute, die in den entlegensten Gegenden der Welt das Unmögliche möglich machen, dann hätte ihn Gisela von Schenk bekommen. Dafür beispielsweise, dass sie im tropischen Dschungel von Peru ein Haus mit Möbeln einrichtete, die es dort nicht gab, mit Gegenständen, die andere für Gerümpel hielten, mit Stoffen, die noch nie jemand in diesem Land gesehen hatte. Ihr Mann zitterte damals, wenn sie mal wieder in vergessenen Gegenden auf der Suche nach originellem Mobiliar war. Als die Einrichtung endlich komplett war, wurden von Schenks vom Militärregime enteignet, zogen zuerst nach New York und kehrten später nach Europa zurück. Seit zwei Jahren lebt von Schenk wieder in ihrer Geburtsstadt Berlin. Zusammen mit Frank Stüve zeigt sie in einer eleganten Grunewald-Villa Interiorkonzepte. »Die Leichtigkeit des Seins« hat sie als Motto über ihre eigene Einrichtung gestellt: »Ich fühle mich zu Hause wie in einem Nest.«

Si l'on récompensait les gens qui réalisent l'impossible dans les endroits situés au diable vert – la palme serait sans nul doute décernée à Gisela von Schenk. Par exemple, pour la maison qu'elle a aménagée dans la jungle péruvienne avec des meubles qui n'existaient pas là-bas, avec des objets que certains considéraient comme du bric-à-brac, avec des tissus inédits dans ce pays. A l'époque, son mari tremblait quand elle partait une fois de plus à la recherche de meubles originaux dans des endroits perdus. Quand la maison fut enfin aménagée comme elle le voulait, les von Schenk furent expropriés par le régime militaire et vécurent un temps à New York avant de rentrer en Europe. Depuis deux ans, Gisela von Schenk vit à nouveau à Berlin, la ville qui l'a vue naître. Avec Frank Stüve, elle présente des idées d'intérieurs dans son élégante villa de Grunewald. Son intérieur à elle est placé sous le signe de «La légèreté de l'être»: «Je me sens chez moi comme dans un nid.»

Rechts: *Gisela von Schenk bewirtet ihre Gäste am französischen Esstisch von Modénature, deren elegante Möbel sie besonders liebt. Im Hintergrund zwei Bilder von Larry Rivers.*
Unten: *Zeichnungen der jungen Berliner Künstlerin Bettina Khano. Über dem neobarocken Sofa von Chelini hängt ein Bild von Johann Erdmann Hummel, einem Wegbereiter der realistischen Malerei.*

Right: *Gisela von Schenk entertains guests at a French dining table by Modénature, whose stylish furniture she is especially attached to. In the background are two pictures by Larry Rivers.*
Below: *drawings by young Berlin artist Bettina Khano. Over the neo-baroque sofa by Chelini hangs a painting by Johann Erdmann Hummel, a precursor of realist art.*

A droite: *Gisela von Schenk restaure ses convives à la table française de Modénature, dont elle apprécie les meubles élégants. A l'arrière-plan, deux tableaux de Larry Rivers.*
Ci-dessous: *des dessins de la jeune artiste berlinoise Bettina Khano. Au-dessus du canapé néo-baroque de Chelini, un tableau de Johann Erdmann Hummel, un pionnier de la peinture réaliste.*

Oben und rechts: Gisela von Schenk wollte »die Leichtigkeit des Seins« in ihre Wohnung bringen. Dazu tragen die hellen Farben des Teppichs und der Möbel bei. Von den weißen Sofas und den tauben-blauen Sesseln aus schaut man durch große Dachfenster in den Himmel Berlins – oder auf die Bilder von Johann Erdmann Hummel.
Folgende Doppelseite: Die große, südländisch wirkende Terrasse hat Frank Stüve mit Sommerblumen und winterhartem Efeu bepflanzt, der das ganze Jahr grün ist.

Above and right: Gisela von Schenk's aim was to introduce "the lightness of being" to her home. The light colours of the carpet and furniture serve this aim. The white settees and pigeon-blue armchairs afford views, through the large skylights, of the Berlin sky – or of paintings by Johann Erdmann Hummel.
Following pages: The large terrace, planted by Frank Stüve with flowers for summer and ivy for winter, has a southern feel to it, and is green all year round.

Ci-dessus et à droite: La moquette et les meubles de couleur claire contribuent à générer la «légèreté de l'être». Assis dans les canapés blancs ou les fauteuils bleu pigeon, on regarde les tableaux de Johann Erdmann Hummel ou le ciel berlinois par la grande lucarne.
Double page suivante: Sur la grande terrasse aux accents méridionaux, Frank Stüve a planté des fleurs d'été et du lierre qui reste vert toute l'année.

His first home is his salon. Udo Walz spends 12 hours of every day there. His second is the Paris Bar. But his favourite is his apartment – a stone's throw from his place of work and from the bar. Berlin's most renowned hairdresser lives right at the top, in an extended rooftop apartment with a terrace. It's too big for one who invariably eats out, but on the other hand it's just big enough for his monthly parties and for his "great passion", moving the furniture around. "If I hadn't become a hairdresser, I'd have chosen interior design as my profession," says Walz. He moved to Berlin in 1967, since it was possible at that time to avoid West German military service by doing so. And so he opted for washing, cutting and styling, and has cared for the hair of Romy Schneider, Claudia Schiffer and Maria Callas. Anyone can get an appointment with the master, though. At times Walz is away, and mostly that means he's at a flea market. "To my way of thinking, living is not a matter of money but of taste."

Udo Walz

Sein erstes Zuhause ist sein Salon, denn da verbringt Udo Walz jeden Tag 12 Stunden. Sein zweites ist die Paris Bar, aber sein liebstes Zuhause ist seine Wohnung – einen Katzensprung vom Arbeitsplatz und von der Bar entfernt. Ganz oben wohnt Berlins bekanntester Friseur, in einem ausgebauten Dachgeschoss mit zwei Terrassen. Zu groß für einen, der eigentlich immer auswärts isst, aber gerade groß genug für die monatlichen Feste und für seine »große Leidenschaft«, Möbel zu rücken. »Wäre ich nicht Friseur geworden, ich hätte die Innenarchitektur zum Beruf gemacht«, sagt Walz. 1967 kam er nach Berlin, weil er nicht zur Bundeswehr wollte. Er entschied sich fürs Waschen, Schneiden, Legen, frisierte die Haare von Romy Schneider, Claudia Schiffer und Maria Callas. Aber einen Termin kriegt jeder beim Meister. Manchmal verreist Walz und fast immer geht er dann zum Trödelmarkt. »Wohnen ist für mich keine Frage des Geldes, sondern des Geschmacks.«

Son domicile numéro un est son salon, vu qu'il y passe 12 heures par jour, le numéro deux étant le Paris Bar. Mais c'est quand même chez lui qu'il se sent le mieux – à deux pas de son travail et du bar. Le coiffeur le plus connu de Berlin habite en hauteur, dans un appartement sous les toits avec terrasse. En principe trop vaste pour quelqu'un qui ne prend jamais ses repas chez lui, mais à peine suffisant pour les fêtes qu'il donne tous les mois et pour sa «grande passion» – déplacer les meubles. «Si je n'étais pas devenu coiffeur, j'aurais choisi l'architecture intérieure», dit Walz. Venu à Berlin en 1967 parce qu'il ne voulait pas faire son service militaire, il se mit au shampooing, à la coupe et à la mise en plis, coiffa Romy Schneider, Claudia Schiffer ou Maria Callas. Mais tout le monde peut prendre rendez-vous avec lui. Walz voyage de temps en temps et va alors presque toujours chiner aux Puces. «L'intérieur pour moi, ce n'est pas une question d'argent mais de goût.»

Rechts: Wohnzimmer und Essbereich gehen ineinander über. Zwei Terrassen gibt es – eine davon mit Morgensonne.
Unten: Udo Walz liebt kräftige Farben. Die roten Wände werden allerdings immer wieder von hellen Farben eingefasst und aufgelockert. Im Sommer lädt Walz seine Gäste am liebsten auf die Terrassen, im Winter brennt auf jeden Fall das Kaminfeuer.

Right: The living room and dining area meet seamlessly. There are two terraces, one with sunshine in the morning.
Below: Udo Walz loves strong colours. Still, the red walls are repeatedly relieved by lighter colours. In the summer Walz likes to ask guests out onto the terraces, while in winter he has a roaring fire burning in the hearth.

A droite: Le séjour et la salle à manger ne sont pas séparés. Il y a deux terrasses, dont l'une reçoit le soleil matinal.
Ci-dessous: Udo Walz aime les couleurs vives. Néanmoins les murs rouges sont toujours encadrés de couleurs claires, ce qui anime l'ensemble. En été, Walz invite volontiers sur les terrasses, en hiver le feu brûle dans la cheminée.

Oben: Von einem strengen, einheitlichen Einrichtungsstil hält Walz nichts, er ergänzt seine Einrichtung lieber mit Gegenständen, die er auf Antik- und Flohmärkten findet.
Rechts: Den Paravent hinter dem roten Sessel hat Walz selbst entworfen und anfertigen lassen.
Folgende Doppelseite: Liebevoll platziert Walz die Wohnaccessoires, deckt persönlich den Tisch für Gäste und setzt Akzente durch Licht.

Above: Udo Walz has no time for austerity or homogeneity in the style of an interior. He prefers to add items found at antique sales or flea markets to his home design.
Right: The screen behind the red armchair was designed by Walz and made to his instructions.
Following pages: Udo Walz positions features with loving care, personally sets the table for his guests, and uses light to discreet effect.

Ci-dessus: Walz ne fait pas grand cas d'un mobilier sévère et homogène; il préfère les objets qu'il trouve chez les antiquaires ou aux Puces.
A droite: Walz a dessiné lui-même le paravent qui se trouve derrière le fauteuil rouge.
Double page suivante: Walz dispose les accessoires avec amour, dresse personnellement la table pour ses invités et pose des accents lumineux.

Michael Haberkorn of Berlin never dreamt of a houseboat. What he'd have liked in the 1970s was a summerhouse in a garden. What he bought instead, for 2,000 deutschmarks, was an old boat. "Not for the romance," says the Green politician; "it was pure chance." He spent a first three years living aboard his boat, and then, after an intermezzo on terra firma, Haberkorn just had to return to a life on the ocean wave, or rather, the wavelets of a canal right by Strasse des 17. Juni. For 12 years, Haberkorn has owned his own houseboat: 65 square metres of the idyllic life, right in the heart of the city. He even has a tiny veranda on which the occasional heron takes a rest. Haberkorn has a paddle-boat moored outside for sunset rides on the water past his eleven neighbours. All of them are fixed abodes, so to speak, for none of these houseboats can be used for journeys by water any more. Just once every eight years they make a short trip, when a tug-boat hauls them for a seaworthiness inspection.

Michael Haberkorn

Von einem Hausboot hat Michael Haberkorn nie geträumt, ein Gartenhäuschen hätte der Berliner in den 1970er Jahren gern gehabt. Gekauft hat er stattdessen für 2000 Mark ein altes Boot. »Nicht wegen der Romantik«, sagt der Grünen-Politiker, »sondern aus reinem Zufall.« Drei Jahre wohnte er damals auf dem Schiff. Nach einem Zwischenspiel auf festem Boden zog es ihn wieder auf die schwankenden Planken zurück – auf einen Kanal direkt an der Straße des 17. Juni. Seit 12 Jahren hat Haberkorn sein eigenes Hausboot: 65 Quadratmeter Idylle mitten in der Stadt. Der ehemalige Lastenschieber hat sogar eine winzige Veranda, auf der schon mal ein Reiher Rast macht. Draußen angebunden dümpelt Haberkorns Paddelboot für Fahrten in die untergehende Sonne, vorbei an seinen elf Nachbarn. Alle mit fester Adresse, denn schippern können die Hausboote nicht mehr. Nur alle acht Jahre geht es auf Reise: Dann schiebt ein Motorboot die Häuser zum TÜV.

Au cours des années 1970, Michael Haberkorn rêvait de cabane dans un jardin. Au lieu de cela, il a acheté un vieux bateau pour 2000 marks. «Pas parce que c'était romantique», dit le Vert, «par hasard, tout simplement.» A l'époque, il y a vécu trois ans. Après un intermède sur la terre ferme, il est revenu à ses anciennes amours et s'est installé sur un canal, juste à côté de la rue du 17-juin. Cela fait maintenant 12 ans que notre Berlinois a sa propre péniche aménagée: 65 mètres carrés de paradis au centre de la ville. L'ancien chaland a même une minuscule véranda sur laquelle un héron vient parfois se reposer. Un canot est amarré dehors, Haberkorn s'en sert pour aller faire un tour quand le soleil se couche et passe devant ses onze voisins. Ils ont tous ont un domicile fixe, car les péniches aménagées ne peuvent plus se déplacer aujourd'hui. Excepté un petit voyage tous les huit ans, quand un bateau à moteur emmène les maisons au TÜV – le service de contrôle technique.

Vorhergehende Doppelseite: Riesige Bäume machen die Liegeplätze der 12 Hausboote von der Straße aus unsichtbar, außerdem halten sie den Lärm fern.

Oben und rechts: Im Sommer spielt sich das Leben draußen ab – entweder auf den kleinen Terrassen der Boote oder am Ufer, wo sich einige Bewohner sogar kleine Vorgärten angelegt haben.

Previous pages: Large trees screen the moorings of the 12 houseboats from the road and shield them from traffic noise.

Above and right: In summer, life is led out of doors, either on the boats' small terraces or on the bank, where some residents have even planted humble gardens.

Double page précédente: De la route, des arbres gigantesques dissimulent les 12 péniches aménagées et les isolent du bruit.

Ci-dessus et à droite: En été, les gens vivent dehors – sur les petites terrasses des bateaux ou sur la rive où quelques habitants ont même aménagé de petits jardins.

Oben und rechts: *Der Hausherr singt in einem Soul-Chor, spielt Rockgitarre und ab und zu Klavier. Häufig gibt es Hausmusikabende mit Freunden und einem Nachbarn, der Musiker ist. Dann spielt Haberkorn entweder die normale, die zwölfseitige oder seine Bass-gitarre.*
Rechte Seite: *Den Kaminofen braucht Michael Haberkorn nur für die Gemütlichkeit und Übergangszeiten, für Minustemperaturen hat er eine Ölheizung.*

Above and right: *The master of the house sings in a soul choir and plays rock guitar and occasionally piano. There are frequent musical evenings with friends and a musician neighbour. Haberkorn plays a normal or twelve-string guitar or bass guitar.*
Facing page: *The stove is used only to provide a cosiness factor, when temperatures begin to fall. There is oil central heating for when they dip below zero.*

Ci-dessus et à droite: *Le propriétaire chante dans une chorale de jazz, joue de la guitare rock et quelquefois du piano. Il y a souvent des soirées musicales avec des amis et un voisin musicien. Haberkorn joue alors de la guitare classique, à douze cordes ou basse.*
Page de droite: *Le poêle ne sert qu'à la mi-saison et parce qu'il ré-pand une douce chaleur; quand il gèle, un chauffage au fioul prend le relais.*

Molly Luft describes herself as "the fattest whore in Germany". And she has also been the best known ever since she paid 10,000 deutschmarks for a giant marble penis in an auction on the TV erotica show "Wahre Liebe". The proceeds went to assist AIDS victims, the penis landed in a brothel, and Molly was all over the press. It was good for business, which in her case is done discreetly in a respectable apartment block in Bambergerstrasse. The doorbell rings, the price is briefly discussed: a quickie costs 25 euros, special wishes are met from 55 up, all according to the price list. Molly's is clean, quiet and orderly. Her brothel opens at ten and closes at seven, every day. On Tuesday evenings Molly goes to the Offener Kanal to do her live broadcast, but the rest of the time she stays at home. For 19 years she has lived at her place of work. She does not consider the way she has done it up appealing, but it serves its purpose: the dark curtain, for instance, separates the "dominant" section. Mostly she is in bed at nine, dreaming of her holiday flat in the traditional old German style.

Molly Luft

Nach eigenen Angaben ist Molly Luft »die dickste Hure Deutschlands«. Und sie ist die bekannteste, seit sie in der Fernsehsendung »Wahre Liebe« für 10 000 Mark einen riesigen Marmorpenis ersteigerte. Der Erlös ging an die Aidshilfe, der Penis in den Puff und Molly kam in die Presse. Gut fürs Geschäft, das im bürgerlichen Mietshaus in der Bambergerstraße diskret abgewickelt wird. Es klingelt, kurze Verhandlung, Schnell-Verkehr für 25, Besonderheiten ab 55 Euro laut Preisliste. Bei Molly geht es sauber, leise und korrekt zu. Ihr Puff öffnet Punkt zehn und schließt um sieben, jeden Tag. Dienstagabends geht Molly für ihre Livesendung zum Offenen Kanal, ansonsten bleibt sie zu Hause. Seit 19 Jahren wohnt sie an ihrem Arbeitsplatz. Nicht schön, aber zweckmäßig findet sie ihre Einrichtung, den dunklen Vorhang beispielsweise, der die Abteilung »dominant« separiert. Meistens liegt sie um neun im Bett und träumt von ihrer Ferienwohnung im altdeutschen Stil.

Molly Luft, ce sont ses propres termes, est «la plus grosse pute d'Allemagne», et aussi la plus connue depuis qu'elle a acheté aux enchères pour 10 000 marks dans l'émission télévisée «Wahre Liebe» un phallus en marbre monumental. L'argent a été versé à l'entraide au Sida, l'objet s'est retrouvé au bordel et Molly dans les journaux. C'est bon pour les affaires qui se font discrètement dans une maison bourgeoise de la Bambergerstrasse où Molly habite depuis 19 ans. On sonne, on discute des tarifs, 25 euros la passe, spécialités à partir de 55 euros. La maison est ouverte tous les jours de dix heures à 19 heures, ici tout est propre, feutré, correct. Le mardi soir, Molly sort car c'est le jour de son émission en direct sur Offener Kanal, sinon elle reste chez elle. Son intérieur, elle ne le trouve pas beau mais pratique, par exemple le rideau sombre qui dissimule l'espace «domination». La plupart du temps, elle se couche tôt et rêve de sa maison de vacances, style néogothique allemand.

Linke Seite: *perfekte 1960er Jahre.*
Oben: *Zimmer Nr. 7 hat einen Kachelofen von 1895 und Original-tapeten von 1950.*
Rechts: *der Eingang zur Acht-Zimmer-Pension.*
Folgende Doppelseite: *das Hochzeitszimmer mit romantischer Rosentapete und Möbeln aus den 1920er Jahren.*
Seite 253: *früheres Gemeinschaftsbad im Flur mit einer alten Waage.*

Facing page: *This is the 1960s to perfection.*
Above: *Room no. 7 has a tiled stove dating from 1895 and original 1950 wallpaper.*
Right: *the entrance to the eight-room pension.*
Following pages: *The bridal room with romantic rose wallpaper and the 1920s suite of furniture.*
Page 253: *The bathroom, with its old scales, was common to all guests.*

Page de gauche: *la perfection des années 1960.*
Ci-dessus: *Dans la chambre n° 7, le poêle date de 1895 et le papier peint des années 1950.*
A droite: *l'entrée de la pension.*
Double page suivante: *La chambre des mariés avec du papier peint romantique et des meubles des années 1920.*
Page 253: *l'ancienne salle de bains commune avec une vieille balance.*

Every Sunday afternoon, Nicolaus Sombart's apartment becomes a salon. The sociologist and writer rejoices in bringing people together, the young and the old, the beautiful and the important, representing the sciences and the arts, from every nation under the sun. Sombart himself is modest. "My function is one of service. I have to ensure that my guests are not bored." Sombart loves this form of social life, and he delights in a gathering freshly assembled – in contrast to "the travelling circus of the smart set". No wonder, for the Berlin-born Sombart grew up in the haute bourgeoisie, and his roots later opened the best of doors in Paris and Rome to him. For 30 years Sombart lived elsewhere, returning only in 1984, "though Berlin – unlike Paris – is not an erotic city," as he puts it. But thanks to his "capacity for enthusiasm" and his favourite virtue, "curiosity", he has discovered other advantages to being in Berlin. Such as the company.

Nicolaus Sombart

An jedem Sonntagnachmittag wird die Wohnung von Prof. Dr. Nicolaus Sombart zum Salon. Menschen will der Soziologe und Schriftsteller zusammenbringen, junge und alte, schöne und bedeutende, aus Wissenschaft und Kunst und aus allen Nationen. Er selbst gibt sich bescheiden. »Ich habe eine dienende Funktion, ich muss dafür sorgen, dass meine Gäste sich nicht langweilen.« Sombart liebt diese Form der Geselligkeit und die frisch gemischte Gesellschaft – nicht »den Wanderzirkus der Schickeria«. Kein Wunder, denn der geborene Berliner wuchs in der Welt des Großbürgertums auf und seine Herkunft öffnete ihm später die Türen der ersten Häuser in Paris und Rom. 30 Jahre lang lebte Sombart anderswo, erst 1984 kehrte er zurück, »obwohl Berlin – im Gegensatz zu Paris – keine erotische Stadt ist«, sagt er. Aber Dank seiner »Begeisterungsfähigkeit« und seiner Lieblingstugend »Neugierde« hat er in Berlin andere Vorzüge entdeckt. Nette Gesellschaft zum Beispiel.

Tous les dimanches après-midi, l'appartement de Nicolaus Sombart se transforme en salon où l'on cause. L'écrivain et sociologue veut rapprocher les jeunes et les vieux, les beaux et les grands de la science et de l'art et de toutes les nationalités. Lui-même fait montre d'humilité. «Ma fonction est de servir, de veiller à ce que mes invités ne s'ennuient pas.» Sombart aime cette forme de vie sociale et il apprécie ce mélange tout frais – pas le «cirque ambulant des gens chics». Rien d'étonnant à cela, vu que ce Berlinois de naissance a vu le jour dans la grande bourgeoisie et que son origine lui a plus tard ouvert les portes des meilleures maisons de Paris et de Rome. 30 ans durant, Sombart a vécu ailleurs, il n'est revenu qu'en 1984, «bien que Berlin – contrairement à Paris –, ne soit pas une ville érotique». Mais grâce à sa capacité d'enthousiasme et sa qualité préférée, la curiosité, il a découvert que Berlin avait quelques autres avantages. Une société agréable, par exemple.

Links: Das »Berliner Zimmer« ist holzgetäfelt und dunkelgrün ge-
strichen. Sonntags wird hier der Tee serviert.
Unten: Vom Eingangsflur gehen die Türen zum Arbeits-, Schlafzim-
mer und zum Salon ab.
Rechte Seite: Alltags nutzt Sombart die Nische mit der Liegestatt im
»Berliner Zimmer« zum Lesen und Fernsehen.

Left: The "Berlin Room" is wood-panelled and painted dark green.
On Sundays tea is served here.
Below: From the hallway the doors open onto the study, bedroom
and salon.
Facing page: For everyday purposes, the recliner corner of the "Berlin
Room" is Sombart's favourite for reading and watching television.

A gauche: La «pièce berlinoise» est lambrissée et peinte en vert sapin.
Le dimanche, on y sert le thé.
Ci-dessous: Les portes du couloir s'ouvrent sur le bureau, la chambre
à coucher et le salon.
Page de droite: Quand il ne reçoit pas, Sombart lit et regarde la télé-
vision du divan encastré dans la niche.

Eingangsseite: Der Stammsessel Sombarts steht nicht im Zentrum
seines Salons, sondern bescheiden in der Ecke nahe der Schiebetür.
Trotzdem steht Sombart im Mittelpunkt der Gesellschaft, denn er
sorgt dafür, dass die Gespräche in Gang kommen und seine Gäste
sich nicht langweilen.
Vorhergehende Doppelseite: Dunkle Wände voller Erinnerungen,
roter Plüsch, Marmorsäulen und Bücher, überall Bücher. Die Salons
des Weltmannes Sombart, der schöne Frauen, bedeutende Männer
und die Gesellschaft liebt, werden nicht durch die übliche Schiebetür,
sondern durch zwei Marmorsäulen getrennt.

First page: Sombart's favourite chair is not in the centre of his salon
but in a modest corner by the sliding door. Sombart is nonetheless the
hub of his social gatherings, ensuring that conversations get going
and his guests are not bored.
Previous pages: dark walls full of memories, red plush, marble columns, and books everywhere. Sombart is a man of the world with a
love of beautiful women, important men, and society. His salons are
divided not by the usual sliding door but by two marble columns.

Première page: Le siège préféré du maître de maison se dresse mo-
destement près de la porte à glissières. Cela n'empêche pas Sombart
de veiller à ce que les conversations aillent bon train et que ses invités
ne s'ennuient pas.
Double page précédente: souvenirs sur les murs sombres, velours
rouge, colonnes de marbre et livres, partout des livres. Deux colonnes
de marbre séparent les salons de notre homme du monde, qui aime
les femmes, les hommes importants et la bonne compagnie.

Berlin Interiors   Nicolaus Sombart

In 1996 Yehuda Teichtal was sent from New York to Berlin as rabbi of the Jewish community and as director of Chabad Lubawitsch, a Hassidic movement. It was not easy for him to go to Germany. His grandfather's family were all killed in the Shoah. But now Teichtal likes it there, because the 4,000 families of the community need him. His especial concern is for Russian immigrants, who were not allowed to observe Jewish customs and who have to begin by learning German. And also for the old people and children. "My wife Leah and I are always on duty," says Teichtal. Duties include Sunday school, holiday camps, parties, seminars and extra tuition. Or entertaining guests at home. The rabbi, born in 1972 in Brooklyn, feels something like a PR manager for the Jewish faith. "To revive a tradition in Berlin and give it a future is of extreme importance for Jewish life," says Teichtal.

Yehuda Teichtal

1996 wurde Yehuda Teichtal als Rabbiner der Jüdischen Gemeinde und als Direktor von Chabad Lubawitsch, einer chassidischen Bewegung, von New York nach Berlin geschickt. Es ist ihm nicht leicht gefallen, nach Deutschland zu gehen, denn die Familie seines Großvaters wurde in der Shoah ermordet. Aber jetzt ist Teichtal gern da, weil die 4000 Familien in der Gemeinde ihn brauchen. Er kümmert sich besonders um die russischen Einwanderer, die jüdische Bräuche nicht pflegen durften und erst mal Deutsch lernen. Und um die Alten und Kinder. »Mein Weib Leah und ich sind immer im Einsatz«, sagt Teichtal. Im Einsatz für die Sonntagsschule, für Ferienlager, Feste, Seminare und Nachhilfeunterricht. Oder zu Hause, wenn sie Gäste bewirten. Ein bisschen fühlt sich der 1972 in Brooklyn geborene Rabbi als PR-Manager des jüdischen Glaubens. »Eine Tradition in Berlin wieder zum Leben zu bringen und weiterzuführen ist extrem wichtig für jüdisches Leben«, sagt Teichtal.

Yehuda Teichtal, rabbin de la communauté juive de New York et directeur de la Beth Loubavitch, un mouvement hassidique, a été envoyé à Berlin en 1996. La famille de son grand-père n'ayant pas survécu à la Shoah, il lui en a coûté de partir en Allemagne. Aujourd'hui pourtant, Teichtal est content d'être ici parce que les 4000 familles de la communauté ont besoin de lui. Il s'occupe surtout des immigrés russes qui n'avaient pas le droit de se conformer aux traditions juives et qui doivent commencer par apprendre l'allemand. Et des vieillards et des enfants. «Ma femme Leah et moi-même, nous sommes toujours occupés», dit-il. Car il y a l'école juive, les colonies de vacances, les fêtes, les séminaires et les cours de rattrapage – et aussi la maison, quand ils accueillent des invités. Le rabbin, né en 1972 à Brooklyn, se sent un peu comme un spécialiste en communications. «Faire revivre une tradition à Berlin et la poursuivre est extrêmement important pour la vie juive», dit Teichtal.

Schöneberg & Tempelhof

People like Olaf Lemke normally exist only in novels: connoisseurs
with real knowledge and experience, specialists who bring passion
and devotion to their pursuits, collectors who have both patience and
a moral sense. Olaf Lemke deals in antique frames, and is one of
twenty such dealers worldwide. He has 2,500 frames in his gallery,
dating from the Renaissance, the Baroque and Rococo, and from the
Neo-Classical and Biedermeier periods. He learnt the trade of gilding,
and it took him a long time and he travelled thousands of kilometres
to acquire his treasures. His travels took him to Catholic countries,
where there are so many saints in need of framing. Lemke spent
many an hour in junk shops till at last he would see a gleam of leaf
gold beneath the dirt on a wooden frame. Back at home he lovingly
restored his finds. And now, when he entertains guests or advises
clients at his refectory table, he can tell tales for hours about every
one of his frames.

Olaf Lemke

Eigentlich gibt es nur noch in Romanen solche Leute wie Olaf
Lemke: Kenner mit Wissen und Erfahrung, Spezialisten mit Leidenschaft und Passion, Sammler mit Geduld und Moral. Olaf Lemke
ist Händler für antike Rahmen, einer von 20 weltweit. 2500 Rahmen
hat er in seiner Galerie, aus der Renaissance, dem Barock, dem
Rokoko, aus dem Klassizismus und dem Biedermeier. Der gelernte
Vergolder hat lange gebraucht, um seine Schätze zusammenzutra-
gen, und er ist dafür Tausende Kilometer gefahren. In katholische
Länder, weil es da so viele Heilige gab, die gerahmt werden muss-
ten. Stundenlang hat Lemke bei Trödlern herumgesucht, bis er beispielsweise unter dem Schmutz einer Holzleiste Blattgold durch-
schimmern sah. Zu Hause restauriert er liebevoll seine Fundstücke.
Wenn er dann an seinem Refektoriumstisch Gäste bewirtet oder
Kunden berät, wird es oft spät, denn Lemke kann stundenlang
Geschichten über jeden Rahmen erzählen.

A vrai dire, des gens comme Olaf Lemke – des connaisseurs disposant
de savoir et d'expérience, des spécialistes pleins d'enthousiasme et de
passion, des collectionneurs patients et scrupuleux – n'existent plus
que dans les romans. Olaf Lemke est l'un des 20 commerçants dans
le monde à vendre des cadres anciens. Sa galerie abrite 2500 cadres
datant des époques Renaissance, baroque, rococo, néoclassique et
Biedermeier. Il a appris le métier de doreur et mis longtemps à ras-
sembler ces trésors. Pour cela, il a dû parcourir des milliers de kilo-
mètres, surtout dans les pays catholiques où il y avait tant de saints
à encadrer. Lemke passait des heures à fouiner chez les brocanteurs
jusqu'à ce qu'il voit scintiller de l'or en feuille sous la saleté recouvrant
le bois. Chez lui, il restaure ses trouvailles avec amour. Quand il invite
à sa table ou donne des conseils à ses clients, le temps semble passer
très vite car il est intarissable sur ses cadres et peut en parler pendant
des heures.

Vorhergehende Doppelseite: *Jeder Zentimeter in der Drei-Zimmer-Wohnung und auf dem kleinen Balkon ist optimal genutzt.*
Oben: *minimalistisches Schlafzimmer.*
Rechts: *eine Teddysammlung und die Hemd-Installation »Ich Metamorphose« von Bruno Nagel, dazu eine kleine Typo-Arbeit von Me Raabenstein.*
Rechte Seite: *zwei gegeneinander gestellte Regale im Schlafzimmer, Fotos von Isabel Simon auf Staffeleien.*

Previous pages: *Every millimetre in this three-room apartment, including the small balcony, is used to best advantage.*
Above: *the minimalist bedroom.*
Right: *a collection of teddy bears, and the shirt installation "Ich Metamorphose" by Bruno Nagel, with a small typographical work by Me Raabenstein.*
Facing page: *back-to-back shelf units in the bedroom, photographs by Isabel Simon on stands.*

Double page précédente: *Le moindre centimètre du trois pièces et du petit balcon est utilisé de manière optimale.*
Ci-dessus: *la chambre à coucher minimaliste.*
A droite: *une collection d'ours en peluche et l'installation de chemises «Ich Metamorphose» de Bruno Nagel, à côté un petit travail typographique de Me Raabenstein.*
Page de droite: *deux étagères l'une contre l'autre dans la chambre à coucher. Sur des chevalets, les photographies d'Isabel Simon.*

As a girl she always wanted to know things, says Edith Lohse. And she loved reading, for preference Russian literature. It turned out a love for life, and took Edith Lohse at the age of 70 to the Soviet Union, from Kiev to Odessa, to the grave of Chekhov and to his white villa at Yalta. She is particularly fond of his melancholy plays about un-lived lives and missed opportunities. Perhaps because there are times when Edith Lohse too wonders if she did everything right in her 90-year life. Education, marriage at 24, three children, any number of grandchildren. She has looked after them all, and has always worked. "And quite right too," she declares roundly. She also thinks it was right to move to Berlin on account of her daughter almost 30 years ago. First she took a furnished flat, but because she likes her own way, Edith Lohse speedily took an apartment she could furnish with her own Bauhaus furniture. "My father gave me these pieces as a wedding present," she recalls with pride.

Edith Lohse

Als Kind, sagt Edith Lohse, sei sie immer wissbegierig gewesen. Und sie las gern, am liebsten russische Literatur. Daraus entstand eine Liebe fürs Leben und deshalb fuhr Edith Lohse als 70-Jährige in die Sowjetunion, von Kiew bis Odessa, an Tschechows Grab und nach Jalta in seine weiße Villa. Besonders schätzt sie seine melancholischen Dramen von versäumten Leben und verpassten Chancen. Vielleicht deshalb, weil sich Edith Lohse auch manchmal fragt, ob sie alles richtig gemacht hat in ihrem 90-jährigen Leben. Ausbildung, Heirat mit 24, drei Kinder, viele Enkel. Um alle hat sie sich gekümmert und immer gearbeitet. »Das war richtig so«, sagt sie dann resolut. Auch, dass sie vor fast 30 Jahren wegen ihrer Tochter nach Berlin kam. Damals wohnte sie zuerst möbliert, aber weil sie am liebsten unabhängig ist, mietete sich Edith Lohse schnell eine Wohnung, mit ihren eigenen Möbeln im Bauhausstil. »Die hat mein Vater mir zur Hochzeit geschenkt«, sagt sie stolz.

Toute petite, dit Edith Lohse, elle était déjà avide d'apprendre. Et elle aimait lire, surtout la littérature russe. La Russie devint son grand amour et à 70 ans, Edith Lohse partit pour l'Union soviétique, voyagea de Kiev à Odessa, alla visiter le tombeau de Tchekhov et sa villa blanche de Yalta. Elle apprécie particulièrement ses drames mélancoliques de vies ratées et de chances négligées. Peut-être parce qu'il lui arrive parfois à 90 ans, de passer sa vie en revue. Formation, mariage à 24 ans, trois enfants, de nombreux petits-enfants. Elle s'est occupée de tous et a toujours travaillé. «C'était bien comme ça», dit-elle alors résolument. Elle n'a jamais regretté non plus de s'être installée à Berlin il y a près de 30 ans à cause de sa fille. A l'époque, elle a d'abord habité dans un logement meublé, mais son indépendance lui tenant à cœur, elle a rapidement loué un appartement et y a installé ses meubles style Bauhaus. «Le cadeau de mariage de mon père», dit-elle fièrement.

Vorhergehende Doppelseite: Familiengeschichte und persönliche Erinnerungen: Edith Lohse mit ihrem Vater, die geliebte Tante Martha, die fromme Tante und die Großmutter vom Bodensee.
Oben: Den runden Esstisch und den Schrank bekam sie als Aussteuer zur Hochzeit vom Vater. Beide Möbel haben jeden Umzug von Edith Lohse mitgemacht.
Rechts: Mitbringsel von ihren vielen Reisen und Familienfotos.
Rechte Seite: Über dem Sofa hängen Gemälde der Tochter Adelheid.

Previous pages: family history and personal memories: Edith Lohse with her father, her dearly-loved Aunt Martha, the pious aunt who became an abbess, and Lohse's Lake Constance grandmother.
Above: The round table and the cupboard were Edith Lohse's dowry, a gift from her father. Both items have moved with Lohse wherever she has gone.
Right: souvenirs of her many travels, and family photos.
Facing page: Above the sofa are paintings by her daughter Adelheid.

Double page précédente: souvenirs de famille: Edith Lohse avec son père, Martha la tante chérie qui devint abbesse et la grand-mère du lac de Constance.
Ci-dessus: La table ronde et l'armoire sont un cadeau de son père, et l'ont accompagnée au cours de tous ses déménagements.
A droite: souvenirs des nombreux voyages et photos de famille.
Page de droite: sur le mur, des tableaux de sa fille Adelheid.

Oben und rechts: Das Schlafzimmer geht auf einen kleinen Balkon, den Edith Lohse liebevoll bepflanzt und pflegt.
Rechte Seite: Alle Bücher über Russland liest Lohse mit Begeisterung. Der größte aller Schriftsteller ist für sie allerdings Anton Tschechow. Auch an der Entwicklung des heutigen Russlands ist sie interessiert – keine Fernsehreportage über ihr Lieblingsland entgeht ihr.
Folgende Doppelseite: Die Keramiken sind Souvenirs aus Italien. Sicherungskasten und Stromzähler verbirgt Edith Lohse eigentlich hinter einem Vorhang.

Above and right: The bedroom opens onto a small balcony which Edith Lohse lavishes loving care on and enlivens with plants.
Facing page: Lohse still reads any book about Russia with gusto. To her mind, the greatest of all writers was Anton Chekhov. But she takes a lively interest in current developments in Russia, and never misses a television report on her favourite country.
Following pages: The ceramics are souvenirs of Italy. Normally Edith Lohse hides the fuse-box and electricity meter behind a curtain.

Ci-dessus et à droite: La chambre à coucher s'ouvre sur un petit balcon qu'Edith Lohse fleurit avec amour.
Page de droite: Edith raffole des livres sur la Russie, pour elle, Anton Tchekhov est le plus grand. Elle s'intéresse aussi à l'évolution de la Russie actuelle – aucun reportage télévisé s'y rapportant ne lui échappe.
Double page suivante: Les céramiques sont des souvenirs d'Italie. Le compteur et les fusibles sont à vrai dire dissimulés derrière un rideau.

Grunewald & Außenbezirke

In 1925 Bruno Paul designed a two-storey villa on a huge parkland plot in Dahlem, and since 1973 it has belonged to Ewa Marja and Georg Heinrichs. The house is a piece of 1920s architectural history, modern, clearly structured, with a Neo-Classical air. And it is a piece of German history too. Auerbach, who had it built, lived in it for only a short period. The Jewish owners emigrated. Next the house took a prominent Nazi's fancy. Later it belonged to the Berlin Senate, which divided the plot into four parts. A bank bought it, rented it out to a ballet school and subsequently to a philistine who had the library and marble floors taken out and put in dark brown tiles and smoked glass doors. The Heinrichs, both architects, took on the reconstruction, renovation and furnishing of the house – till it was once again a Bruno Paul villa.

Ewa Marja &
Georg Heinrichs

Auf einem großen Parkgrundstück plante Bruno Paul 1925 die Dahlemer Villa, die seit 1973 Ewa Marja und Georg Heinrichs gehört. Das Haus ist ein Stück Baugeschichte der 1920er Jahre, modern und klar gegliedert, mit neoklassischem Einschlag. Und es ist deutsche Geschichte. Bauherr Auerbach bewohnte es nur kurz, die jüdischen Besitzer wanderten aus. Dann gefiel das Haus einer Nazigröße, gehörte später dem Berliner Senat, der das Grundstück viertelte, dann kaufte es eine Bank. Die vermietete es einer Ballettschule und später einem Banausen, der die Bibliothek und Marmorböden rausriss und braune Fliesen und Rauchglastüren einbaute. Das Architekten-Paar Heinrichs rekonstruierte, renovierte und möblierte – bis daraus wieder eine Bruno-Paul-Villa wurde.

Bruno Paul a conçu en 1925 dans un parc immense de Dahlem la villa de deux étages qui appartient depuis 1973 à Ewa Marja et Georg Heinrichs. Moderne et clairement structuré avec une touche néoclassique, c'est un monument de l'architecture des années 1920 et de l'histoire allemande. Auerbach, le maître d'œuvre, n'y habita que peu de temps, les propriétaires juifs émigrèrent. Ensuite, la maison charma un ponte nazi; plus tard elle appartînt au Sénat de Berlin qui fit diviser le terrain en quatre, et la vendit à une banque. Celle-ci la loua à une école de danse et plus tard à un béotien qui fit arracher la bibliothèque et les sols de marbre et installer des carrelages brun foncé et des portes en verre fumé. Les Heinrichs, tous deux architectes, ont travaillé jusqu'à ce que renaisse la villa de Bruno Paul.

Vorhergehende Doppelseite: *Die Grafiken sind von Richard Smith, die Sitzgruppe von Alvar Aalto.*
Oben: *Georg Heinrichs hat in Alvar Aaltos Architekturbüro für die »Interbau« 1956 in Berlin gearbeitet. Sofa, Hocker und auch die Lampe links sind von Aalto. Auch die Aluminium-Stehlampe von Fridtjof Schliephacke ist ein Klassiker.*
Rechte Seite: *Blick auf die Terrasse und den parkartigen Garten.*

Previous pages: *The graphics are by Richard Smith and the chairs by Alvar Aalto.*
Above: *Georg Heinrichs worked in Alvar Aalto's architectural office for "Interbau" 1956 in Berlin. The sofa, stools and lamp to the left are by Aalto. The aluminium standard lamp by Fridtjof Schliephacke is likewise a classic.*
Facing page: *looking onto the terrace and garden.*

Double page précédente: *Les dessins sont signés Richard Smith, les sièges sont d'Alvar Aalto.*
Ci-dessus: *Georg Heinrichs a travaillé dans le cabinet d'architectes d'Alvar Aalto pour l'«Interbau» de Berlin en 1956. Le canapé, les tabourets et la lampe à gauche sont d'Aalto. Le lampadaire en aluminium de Fridtjof Schliephacke est aussi un classique.*
Page de droite: *vue sur la terrasse et le jardin aux airs de parc.*

Oben: *Esstisch mit Stühlen von Marcel Breuer. Vier Stehlampen von Fridtjof Schliephacke beleuchten die Wandmalerei des Amerikaners Ron Davis, der in den 1960er Jahren Perspektiven in abstrakte Gemälde umsetzte.*
Rechts: *Le Corbusier-Sessel und Bauhaus-Schachspiel, zwei zeitlose Klassiker.*

Above: *dining table and chairs by Marcel Breuer. Four standard lamps by Fridtjof Schliephacke light the mural by American artist Ron Davis, who translated perspective studies into abstract paintings in the 1960s.*
Right: *a classic: Le Corbusier armchairs and a Bauhaus chess set.*

Ci-dessus: *table et chaises de Marcel Breuer. Quatre lampadaires de Fridtjof Schliephacke éclairent la peinture murale de l'Américain Ron Davis qui a transformé des perspectives en peintures abstraites au cours des années 1960.*
A droite: *fauteuils Le Corbusier et échiquier Bauhaus – des classiques.*

Berlin Interiors   Ewa Marja & Georg Heinrichs

Rechts: *vier Stühle von Ludwig Mies van der Rohe im Schlafzimmer.*
Unten: *am Kopfende neun Bilder von Robert Mangold, neben dem Bett wieder Klassiker, Beistelltische von Eileen Gray.*

Right: *four chairs by Ludwig Mies van der Rohe in the bedroom.*
Below: *At the head of the bed are nine pictures by Robert Mangold, while the occasional table is another classic, by Eileen Gray.*

A droite: *quatre chaises de Ludwig Mies van der Rohe dans la chambre à coucher.*
Ci-dessous: *sur le mur, neuf tableaux signés Robert Mangold; à côté du lit, classiques ici aussi, des tables de chevet d'Eileen Gray.*

Thomas Herrendorf has a perfectly simple recipe for becoming a successful interior designer: tolerance and cosmopolitan openness. "Anything is possible," says Herrendorf, and that includes his own house too. By the Louis Seize chair is an African table, a precious Venini vase stands beside a ruby-red carafe bought at a flea market. This is neither the product of chance nor creative chaos; Herrendorf's idea of tolerance is a well-considered and exact one. The colours of his bedroom, for instance, are the subdued, chalky hues of a pair of Baroque angels, and when Herrendorf says "mauve" or "sandy" he does not mean "beige" and most assuredly not "the usual champagne aria". He has converted the garage of his Art Nouveau house into a party and cooking space for 25 guests. "It's marvellous," says Herrendorf, "if you can simply walk out after a party, step next door into the house, and wake up next morning without being confronted by all the washing-up."

Thomas Herrendorf

Thomas Herrendorf hat ein einfaches Rezept, wie man ein erfolgreicher Inneneinrichter wird: Toleranz und kosmopolitische Offenheit. »Alles ist möglich«, sagt Herrendorf, natürlich auch in seinem eigenen Haus: Vor dem Louis-Seize-Sessel steht ein afrikanischer Tisch, die kostbare Venini-Vase behauptet sich neben einer rubinroten Karaffe vom Flohmarkt. Zufall oder kreatives Chaos ist das nicht, Herrendorfs Toleranz-Konzept ist überlegt und präzise. Sein Schlafzimmer hat er beispielsweise nach den müden, kalkigen Farben eines barocken Engelpaares konzipiert, und wenn Herrendorf »mauve« und »sandig« sagt, meint er nicht »beige« und schon gar nicht »die übliche Champagner-Arie«. Die Garage neben seinem Jugendstilhaus hat Herrendorf in ein Party- und Küchenhaus für 25 Gäste umgebaut. »Wunderbar«, sagt Herrendorf, »wenn man nach der Feier einfach aufsteht, fünf Schritte ins Wohnhaus geht und am nächsten Morgen nicht den Abwasch vor der Nase hat.«

Pour Thomas Herrendorf avoir du succès comme architecte d'intérieur n'est pas bien sorcier, il suffit d'être tolérant et ouvert sur le monde. «Tout est possible», dit-il, et sa propre demeure lui donne raison: devant le fauteuil Louis XVI se dresse une table africaine; le précieux vase de Venini côtoie une carafe vermeille chinée aux Puces. Il ne s'agit ni de hasard bienveillant ni de chaos créatif, le concept de tolérance cher à Herrendorf se révèle réfléchi et précis. Sa chambre à coucher, par exemple, a été conçue d'après les couleurs crayeuses et passées d'une paire d'angelots baroques, et quand il dit «mauve» et «sable», il ne veut pas dire «beige» et en aucun cas «champagne», trop répandu à son goût. Il a transformé le garage qui annexe sa maison Jugendstil en salle des fêtes avec cuisine pour 25 personnes. «C'est formidable», dit Herrendorf, «de pouvoir aller se coucher à trois pas de là après la fête, sans avoir à contempler la vaisselle sale le lendemain matin.»

Eingangsseite: Der Kronleuchter stammt aus der Residenz des West-
berliner Stadtkommandanten.
Oben: Ohrensessel aus den 1920er Jahren, afrikanischer Hocker, ein
Sofa von Driade und eine Holzsäule aus Indien.
Rechts: auf dem Marmorkamin eine Vasensammlung.
Rechte Seite: Essplatz mit Stühlen von Philippe Starck und einer
Kommode von Mendini. Das Bild »Wasserballer« hat Arthur Kampf
in den 1920er Jahren gemalt.

First page: This chandelier was in the residence of the West Berlin city
commandant.
Above: the wing armchair is 1920s, the stools are African and the
wooden column is Indian.
Right: On the marble mantelpiece is a collection of vases.
Facing page: dining area with chairs by Philippe Starck and a chest
by Mendini. The painting "Wasserballer" was done by Arthur Kampf
in the 1920s.

Première page: Le lustre vient de la résidence du commandant de
place à Berlin-Ouest.
Ci-dessus: fauteuils à oreilles des années 1920, tabourets africains,
oun canapé de Driade et une colonne de bois indienne.
A droite: une collection de vases sur la cheminée.
Page de droite: le coin repas avec des chaises de Philippe Starck et
une commode de Mendini. Le tableau «Wasserballer» des années
1920 est signé Arthur Kampf.

Vorhergehende Doppelseite: Neben die rubinrote Glaskaraffe vom Flohmarkt stellt Herrendorf kostbare Venini-Vasen; im Wintergarten sind noch alte Malereifragmente zu sehen, der Klapp-Spieltisch mit Intarsien kommt aus Syrien.

Oben und rechte Seite: Für sein barockes Engelpaar hat Herrendorf das ganze Schlafzimmer auf die Farben seiner Lieblingsskulpturen abgestimmt.

Rechts: Badekeller mit Sauna, Dusche und Badewanne. Der antike Schinkel-Eisenstuhl passt gut zu den Bodenfliesen aus Terrakotta.

Previous pages: Herrendorf has precious Venini vases alongside a ruby-red carafe found at a flea market. In the winter garden, old fragments of paintings are still to be seen. The collapsible table with inlay is from Syria.

Above and facing page: For his pair of Baroque angels, Herrendorf has matched his whole bedroom to the colours of his favourite sculptures.

Right: the cellarage bathroom with sauna, shower and a bathtub. The antique iron chair by Schinkel goes well with the terracotta floor tiles.

Double page précédente: carafe des Puces et vases de Venini; sur les murs du jardin d'hiver, des traces de fresques peintes, la table à jouer dépliante en marqueterie vient de Syrie.

Ci-dessus et page de droite: A sa paire d'anges baroques Herrendorf a harmonisé sa chambre à coucher à leurs couleurs.

A droite: dans la cave, un sauna, des douches et une baignoire. La chaise en fer ancienne de Schinkel fait bon ménage avec les tomettes.

Berlin Interiors   Thomas Herrendorf

Werner Aisslinger is used to the expectation of visitors, who imagine his house will be furnished in a purist or even futurist style. Because he designs recliners incorporating unusual materials such as gel, or transportable aluminium houses for living on unoccupied rooftops. But the fact of the matter is that Aisslinger doesn't go for the designer look in his own home, but rather for a country house style. "The furniture should always be seen in relation to the architecture," he says, and in any case a house bears the imprint of the family's taste. His wife Nicola Bramigk, a fashion designer, chose the colours, the fabrics and much of the furniture. It was she who brought back the old glass-fronted cabinets from Provence and designed the dining table, at which diners sit on Aisslinger's hit chair "Juli".

Nicola Bramigk & Werner Aisslinger

Werner Aisslinger ist gewohnt, dass Besucher in seinem Haus eine puristische oder sogar futuristische Einrichtung erwarten. Weil er Liegen mit ungewöhnlichen Materialien wie Gel entwickelt oder transportierbare Aluminiumhäuser zum Wohnen auf ungenutzten Hausdächern entwirft. Fehlanzeige, Aisslinger wohnt nicht im Designerlook, sondern eher im Landhausstil. »Die Einrichtung muss man immer in Relation zur Architektur sehen«, sagt er, und außerdem bringe man sich als Familie zusammen ein. Von seiner Frau Nicola Bramigk, einer Modedesignerin, kommen beispielsweise die Farbgebung, die Stoffe und viele Möbel. Sie hat die alten Glasschränke aus der Provence mitgebracht und den Esstisch entworfen, um den Aisslingers Erfolgsstuhl »Juli« steht.

Werner Aisslinger sait que les gens s'attendent à trouver chez lui un intérieur puriste voire minimaliste – il faut dire qu'il élabore des lits en gel, par exemple, et qu'il conçoit des maisons en aluminium transportables que l'on peut placer sur les toits. Ces gens là ont tout faux: Aisslinger n'est pas un adepte du look design, il serait plutôt tendance rustique. «L'intérieur doit toujours être en relation avec l'architecture», dit-il, et puis c'est un choix familial. Les coloris, les tissus et les nombreux meubles, par exemple, sont l'idée de sa femme Nicola Bramigk, styliste de mode. Elle a rapporté les vieilles armoires vitrées de Provence et dessiné la table qui tient compagnie à «Juli», la chaise à succès d'Aisslinger.

Vorhergehende Doppelseite: Nicola Bramigk und Werner Aisslinger teilen sich die alte Villa von 1916 mit Freunden. Sie selbst bewohnen das Erdgeschoss.

Oben und rechts: Stilmix: Am langen, alten Esstisch aus der Provence stehen Werner Aisslingers Stühle »Juli«, die beiden Schränke hat Nicola Bramigk vom großen Antikmarkt in Isle sur la Sorgue mitgebracht.

Previous pages: Nicola Bramigk and Werner Aisslinger share the old villa, built in 1916, with friends. They themselves occupy the ground floor.

Above and right: a mix of styles. Werner Aisslinger's "Juli" chairs are at the long old dining table from Provence. Nicola Bramigk acquired the two cabinets at the great antiques market in Isle sur la Sorgue.

Double page précédente: Nicola Bramigk et Werner Aisslinger partagent la villa de 1916 avec des amis. Eux-mêmes habitent au rez-de-chaussée.

Ci-dessus et à droite: un pot-pourri de styles: près de la table provençale ancienne, les chaises «Juli» de Werner Aisslinger. Nicola Bramigk a rapporté les deux armoires du grand marché à la brocante d'Isle sur la Sorgue.

Rechts und unten: *Die Fuchsfelldecke auf dem modernen Bett stammt von einem Jägerfreund. Auch hier gesellt sich modernes Design, wie die Zuglampen von Achille Castiglioni, zu alten Dingen, wie dem französischen Spiegel.*

Right and below: *The fox fell counterpane on the modern bed came from a hunter friend. Here, too, modern design, such as the lamps by Achille Castiglioni, goes hand in hand with old things such as the French mirror.*

A droite et ci-dessous: *Le dessus-de-lit en renard vient d'un ami chasseur. Ici aussi, le design moderne – les lampes à tirette d'Achille Castiglioni – côtoie les objets anciens, tel le miroir français.*

The owners describe their boathouse as "a place of hospitality, peace and easy living". No wonder, with a house made of white-painted wood, with a shingled roof and a waterside verandah with twining vines. Not that the boathouse was always in such fine form. It is in the park-like grounds of a villa built in 1917, and as the name suggests was used for boats before subsequently being demoted to a lumber room. Only when they vacated the villa did the owners decide to renovate the idyllic boathouse and use it as a weekend retreat. In fact it was completely converted – architect Dieter Mann describes it with amusement as "a high-tech shed". He packed thick insulation wadding between the façade and the planking interior walls, masked all the supports, and devised a clever heating system. Ira Schwarz furnished the house. The name of her country-style furniture shop in Potsdam translates as "Garden dreams" – and the boathouse is a dream come true.

Bootshaus

Als »Ort der Gastlichkeit, der Ruhe und Leichtigkeit« bezeichnen die Besitzer ihr Bootshaus. Kein Wunder bei einem Haus aus weißem Holz mit Schindeldach und einer weinumrankten Veranda, die ins Wasser ragt. So schön war das Bootshaus nicht immer. Es liegt im Garten einer 1917 gebauten Villa und diente als Liegeplatz für Boote. Später wurde es zur Abstellkammer degradiert. Erst beim Auszug aus der Villa entschlossen sich die Besitzer, die kleine Idylle als Wochenendhaus zu nutzen und dafür zu renovieren. Daraus wurde ein kompletter Umbau. Einen »High-Tech-Schuppen« nennt Architekt Dieter Mann amüsiert das Haus. Zwischen Fassade und holzbeplankter Innenwand hat er dicke Wärmedämmung gepackt, alle Stützen ummantelt und eine raffinierte Heizungstechnik ausgetüftelt. Ira Schwarz hat das Haus eingerichtet. Ihr Potsdamer Geschäft mit ländlichen Möbeln heißt »Gartenträume« – das Bootshaus ist ein wahr gewordener Traum.

Les propriétaires estiment que leur maison est un «lieu de convivialité, de calme et de légèreté». Rien d'étonnant, vu qu'elle est en bois blanc, avec un toit de bardeaux et une véranda perdue sous la vigne. Pourtant, elle n'a pas toujours été aussi agréable à regarder. Située dans le parc d'une villa édifiée en 1917, elle a d'abord servi de hangar à bateaux avant de devenir carrément un débarras. Ce n'est qu'en quittant la villa que les propriétaires s'avisèrent qu'elle ferait une charmante maison de week-end et décidèrent de la restaurer. Ce qui déboucha sur une transformation complète. «C'est une bicoque high-tech», plaisante l'architecte Dieter Mann. Entre la façade et le mur intérieur, il a intercalé une épaisse isolation thermique, enveloppé tous les supports et mis au point un système de chauffage raffiné. Ira Schwarz s'est occupée de la décoration intérieure. Son magasin de meubles rustiques à Potsdam s'appelle «Rêves de jardin» – la maison est un rêve devenue réalité.

Eingangsseite: *Kaum zu glauben, dass das weiße Haus mit den Holzschindeln einmal ein Abstellschuppen war. Architekt Dieter Mann hat es außerdem noch technisch perfekt ausgerüstet.*
Vorhergehende Doppelseite und rechts: *Ira Schwarz richtete das Haus mit ländlichen Möbeln und Accessoires aus ihrem Potsdamer Geschäft »Gartenträume« ein.*
Unten: *Das Wochenenddomizil besteht nur aus einem großen Raum mit Duschbad und einer Abstellkammer.*

First page: *It is scarcely believable that this white wooden house was once used as a lumber store. Architect Dieter Mann has revived its fortunes and equipped it with every technical comfort.*
Previous pages and right: *Ira Schwarz furnished the house with country-style furniture and accessories from her shop in Potsdam, the name of which translates as "Garden dreams".*
Below: *The weekend retreat consists of a single large room, with shower and store-room.*

Première page: *Qui croirait que la jolie maison blanche était autrefois un débarras? En outre, elle est parfaitement équipée sur le plan technique, grâce à Dieter Mann.*
Double page précédente et à droite: *Ira Schwarz a meublé et décoré la maison.*
Ci-dessous: *La maison comporte une seule grande pièce avec cabine de douche et débarras.*

Oben: der schönste Aussichtsplatz zu jeder Jahreszeit. Alle Fenster-
türen sind komplett aufzuschieben und Dieter Mann hat sogar Heiz-
strahler über den Sofas an die Decke montieren lassen, falls jemand
bei offenem Fenster frösteln sollte.
Rechts: Die Innenwände sind holzbeplankt.
Folgende Doppelseite: Traumaussicht auf rote Blätter, stahlgraues
Wasser, grünes Ufer – und im Sommer könnte man von der Terrasse
aus direkt ins Wasser springen.

Above: the finest place to enjoy the view at any season of the year.
All the full-length windows slide open, and Dieter Mann has even installed ceiling heaters above the settees in case anyone feels a chill
when the windows are open.
Right: The interior walls are planked.
Following pages: a matchless view of red leaves, steely grey water
and green lake-shore. And in summer you can take a dip from your
own terrace.

Ci-dessus: Les portes-fenêtres sont complètement coulissantes pour
jouir de la vue au fil des saisons. Dieter Mann a même fait installer
des radiateurs électriques au plafond, au-dessus des canapés pour les
personnes frileuses.
A droite: Les murs intérieurs sont lambrissés.
Double page suivante: feuilles rouges, eau couleur de métal, rive
verdoyante – un paysage de rêve – et en été on pourrait directement
plonger dans l'eau.